Denise Monteiro

Value Stream Mapping

Denise Monteiro

Value Stream Mapping

Framework based on a Systematic Literature Review

ScienciaScripts

Imprint
Any brand names and product names mentioned in this book are subject to trademark, brand or patent protection and are trademarks or registered trademarks of their respective holders. The use of brand names, product names, common names, trade names, product descriptions etc. even without a particular marking in this work is in no way to be construed to mean that such names may be regarded as unrestricted in respect of trademark and brand protection legislation and could thus be used by anyone.

Cover image: www.ingimage.com

This book is a translation from the original published under ISBN 978-620-2-19359-7.

Publisher:
Sciencia Scripts
is a trademark of
Dodo Books Indian Ocean Ltd. and OmniScriptum S.R.L publishing group

120 High Road, East Finchley, London, N2 9ED, United Kingdom
Str. Armeneasca 28/1, office 1, Chisinau MD-2012, Republic of Moldova, Europe
Managing Directors: Ieva Konstantinova, Victoria Ursu
info@omniscriptum.com

Printed at: see last page
ISBN: 978-620-7-27961-6

SUMMARY

ACKNOWLEDGMENTS

I thank God for illuminating my path and giving me the strength to move forward with my goals.

I would especially like to thank my parents, Donilha Loyola do Amaral ↑ and Carlos Almir do Amaral ↑, for being my inexhaustible source of energy, for their unconditional love and for being the reason for my constant struggle to become a better person every day. Thank you for the examples of strength and courage that made me never give up on my dreams.

To my beloved husband, Aluisio, for his intense support throughout the process of building this research and for sharing so many other dreams and projects. Without his support, trust and love, I wouldn't have made it this far.

To my much-loved daughter, Esther, for the most sincere and profound love I have ever received. My "little seed" that brought joy, hope and unconditional love into my life. I am eternally grateful and happy to have you.

I would like to thank my advisor Prof. Fernando Luiz Cyrino Oliveira for his great confidence and valuable contributions to this work. I would especially like to thank my co-supervisor Prof. Màrcio Thomé for his great dedication and support. His experience and knowledge, which he passed on throughout the development of this work, were fundamental to its successful completion.

To all the professors at the Department of Industrial Engineering and PUC-RJ for their teaching and guidance, contributing to my evolution and academic development.

To my friends for sharing the anguish and joy with me over the years.

Finally, my deepest thanks to all those who contributed to this research.

SUMMARY

MONTEIRO, Denise Loyola Silva. ***Value Stream Mapping*: A Systematic Literature Review**. Rio de Janeiro, 2015. Master's dissertation (professional option) - Department of Industrial Engineering, Pontifical Catholic University of Rio de Janeiro.

Value Stream Mapping (VSM) is one of the Lean Production tools that has been widely discussed in the literature for mapping production and service processes with a focus on reducing waste and non-value added time. Despite the growing number of publications on the subject, the academic literature shows the absence of systematic research that presents the state of the art. Thus, this research, through a systematic and careful review of the literature, aims to gather information on the VSM in order to identify its main characteristics, trends and opportunities for new developments and future research. The review includes 263 abstracts and 91 articles selected for review and classification. The study proposes a synthesis, in the form of a conceptual frame of reference, which presents how VSM is adopted in certain contexts and motivations, outlining a better understanding of how the tool is implemented and the respective outputs and results that can be generated. It was noted that VSM is spreading rapidly to the service sector, especially *health care* and logistics. However, studies report that implementing VSM in practice is a lengthy process. Problems related to resistance to improvement, involving changes in the workforce and demands on scarce internal resources, have encouraged some researchers to question the use of the tool. This research contributes to a better understanding of the subject and provides pointers for future VSM research and practice.

KEY WORDS

Systematic literature review; conceptual frame of reference; waste reduction.

1. Introduction

The market is undergoing constant transformations that form a new dynamic context for organizations. Companies that conquer faster markets with reduced delivery times, production in small, customized batches and with products that meet customer expectations, create significant competitive leverage (Salgado et al., 2009).

As a result, it is necessary to use lean tool practices to eliminate waste (Marchwinski, 2004), which generates greater flexibility and quality in manufacturing systems. In this context, the philosophy of Lean Production (Womack & Jones, 1996) presents *Value Stream Mapping* (VSM) as a value stream mapping tool (Rother & Shook, 1998; Pavnaskar et al., 2003) that aims to reorganize production systems with a lean vision focused on identifying waste and adding value to the customer.

Unlike most process mapping techniques, which often only document the basic flow of the product, VSM also documents the flow of information within the system, such as the movement of materials, *lead times*, stock levels and resource utilization (Singh et al., 2011). For Womack & Jones (1996), the VSM should be applied as the first step in implementing a new lean production scenario.

Since the application of VSM has been discussed in the literature in recent years (Hines & Rich, 1997; Hines et al., 1998; Sullivan et al., 2002; Lima & Zawslak, 2003; Kaale et al., 2005; Braglia et al., 2006; Adrian et al., 2007; Barber & Tietje, 2008; Al-Tahat, 2010; Lu et al., 2011; Teichgraber & de Bucourt, 2012; Basu & Dan, 2014; Susilawati et al., 2015), with efforts aimed at improving productivity, reducing *lead times* and, in particular, the success of its application (Hines et al., 1999; Lima & Zawslak, 2003; Abdulmalek & Rajgopal, 2007; Lian & Van Landeghem, 2007; Barber & Tietje, 2008; Matt, 2008; Serrano et al., 2008; Salgado et al., 2009; Wang et al., 2009; Chen et al., 2010; Ng et al., 2010; Cima et al., 2011; Cookson et al., 2011; Garrett & Lee, 2011; Gurumurthy & Kodali, 2011; Nepal et al., 2011; Schwarz et al., 2011;

Carter et al, 2012; Duranik et al, 2012; Garg & Naido, 2012; Wong et al, 2012; Chen et al, 2013; Marques et al, 2013; Tanco et al, 2013; Yu et al, 2013; Basu & Dan,

2014; Brown et al, 2014; Cevikcan & Durmusoglu, 2014; Heinzen et al, 2014; Matt, 2014; Tyagi et al., 2014), questions related to the difficulties in implementation, how to obtain maximum performance and how to maintain the gains obtained with such an application (Mohanty et al., 2007; Lasa et al. 2008) are still common.

The lack of complete understanding of the methodology's approach, as well as the lack of understanding of the implementation process on the part of the organization's managers, may be reasons why some companies are unable to maintain continuous improvements (Mohanty et al., 2007). Another important fact is that, in recent years, no document has been published that evaluates and classifies the literature on the VSM (Singh et al., 2011), justifying the lack of systematic reviews on the subject.

In this context and in the absence of systematic reviews on the subject, gathering information so that any professional can evaluate how the tool can be adopted to their reality or offer a better understanding of how the implementation of the VSM is presented, can be useful.

The general aim of this research is to present a systematic review of the literature on the VSM methodology, seeking to identify its main characteristics, trends and opportunities for new developments in future research. The potential gain from studying the VSM methodology in all its aspects brings researchers and professionals in the field benefits, especially with a systematic and careful survey of the subject.

The research can generate appropriate means that lead to benefits such as: *(i)* serving as a basis for greater knowledge of the existing literature on the VSM; *(ii)* knowing the theoretical advances and the level of knowledge in the VSM methodology and; *(iii)* identifying the relevance of the current knowledge base for the VSM.

2. Methodology

The research is a systematic review of the literature on the VSM. A systematic literature review involves a process of objective theoretical evaluation (Hopayian, 2001) with a focus on empirical studies and seeks to summarize previous studies on the topic of interest (Cooper, 2010). This type of evaluation allows conclusions to be drawn from studies that are similar with the aim of presenting the state of the art on the relationships of interest and emphasizing important questions that remain unanswered on a given topic (Cooper, 2010).

Cooper's (2010) seven-step approach was adopted in this research: *(i)* problem formulation; *(ii)* database search; *(iii)* data collection; *(iv)* primary research quality assessment; *(v)* analysis and synthesis; *(vi)* data interpretation; and *(vii)* reporting.

For the execution of step *(ii)*, step *(iii),* step *(iv) of* Cooper (2010) and for the selection and retrieval of documents in the systematic review, a six-step process was adopted adapted from Thomé et al. (2012a), Thomé et al. (2012b) and Thomé et al. (2014): *(i)* selection of the electronic database, *(ii)* identification of the keywords for the search, *(iii)* criteria for excluding studies, *(iv)* manual review of the abstracts of the articles obtained, *(v) review of the* full text of the articles selected, and *(vi)* review of the references selected from the articles retrieved in step v.

Five databases were selected for the research, as they include most of the academic journals referenced in the field of Operations Management, as well as studies and applications originating from industry: EBSCO, ELSEVIER, EMERALD, SCIELO and WILEY.

In accordance with the recommendations for the initial search (Cooper, 2010), the keywords selected were comprehensive for the field of research and specific enough to avoid undesirable results (Thomé et al., 2014). The following phrase was adapted for searching each database: "Value Stream Mapping" OR "Value Stream Map" OR "VSM". The search was carried out using keywords, abstract and title, with no limitations as to the date of the search.

The search covered 263 documents, as detailed in Figure 1.

It can be seen that, in terms of quantity, the EBSCO database stands out with 60% of the results obtained in the searches.

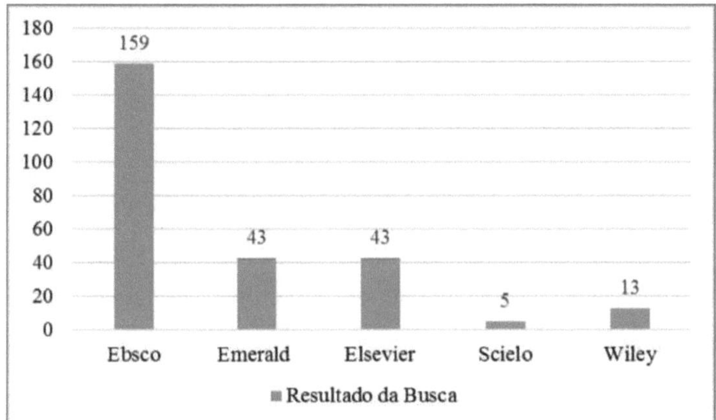

Figure 1 - Results of the search through five databases.

Source: Prepared by the author.

The process of systematically and carefully reviewing the literature on the VSM was interactive and resulted in a high level of agreement.

At first, the criteria for excluding the articles were discussed and defined, as suggested by Cooper (2010): *(i) articles* that use VSM only as an example of a *lean* tool, *(ii)* articles that do not address the entire scope of the VSM process, with application of the technique; *(iii) articles* based only on the author's opinion; *(iv)* articles from commercial magazines, advertising or promoting products and services (*software,* consultancies, etc.) and; (v) articles that present the benefits of VSM without empirical evidence based on case studies, research studies - surveys, mathematical models, action research, review of the benefits of VSM.) and; *(v)* articles presenting the benefits of VSM without empirical evidence based on case studies, research studies - *surveys,* mathematical models, action research, literature reviews or simulations. In addition, the search yielded unwanted results for articles on VSM (*Viable System Model*) and VSM (*Vascular Smooth Muscle*). These articles were excluded and are not included in the list of 263 initial articles.

The 263 abstracts were read and discussed in two meetings which resulted in four reviews. Based on the reading of the abstracts, documents that did not meet the above criteria and duplicate documents (16 articles) were excluded. At this stage, the evaluation of the abstracts was carried out and the reliability process was monitored. It can be compared with the number of articles on VSM found in previous systematic reviews: 91 articles on VSM selected for full-text review against 49 by Singh et al. (2011), 52 by Bhamu & Sangwan (2014) and 47 by Hadid & Mansouri (2014).

It is important to note that unlike Singh et al. (2011), which only looks at the types of studies published on the VSM in recent years, this research looks at the types of studies used in publications on the VSM and synthesizes the literature review based on the development of a *framework*.

The search process showed satisfactory agreement rates from the third review in the screening process, as shown in Table 1.

To this end, *Cohen*'s *Kappa* (K) method was used, based on measuring the degree of agreement between the judges analyzing each individual in a sample on a nominal scale (Fleiss, 1971; Krippendorf, 2004b). *Kappa* (K) measures the degree of agreement beyond what would be expected by chance alone (Fleiss, 1971; Krippendorf, 2004b).

Table 1 - Summary of agreement coefficient results.

		Reviews			
coefficient of agreement		1	2	3	4
Percentage of Concordance in Pairs	Reviewers 1 & 3	84,091	85,171	92.776	93,536
	Reviewers 1 & 2	84,848	90,114	97.719	97,719
	Reviewers 2 & 3	87,879	93,536	93.536	94,297
	Average %	85.606	89.607	94,677	95,184
Fleiss' Kappa	agreement Observed	0,856	0,896	0,947	0,952
	agreement	0,538	0,534	0,522	0,521

	Expected Coefficient	0,689	0,777	0,889	0,899
Percentage in Pairs of Kappa of Cohen	Reviewers 1 & 3	0,638	0,674	0,848	0,864
	Reviewers 1 & 2	0,681	0,799	0,953	0,953
	Reviewers 2 & 3	0,747	0,864	0,864	0,881
	Average %	0,688	0,776	0,866	0,899
Alpha of Krippendorff	N Decisions	789	789	789	789
	N cases	263	263	263	263
	Σo	678	707	747	751
	$\Sigma_{c} n_c(n_c - 1)$	336602	331484	324084	323432
	Coefficient	0,689	0,777	0,889	0,899

Source: Prepared by the author.

A low degree of agreement is obtained in the first meetings, due to different assessments, as can be seen in the percentage of agreement in pairs and in the *Kappa* coefficients. The results are consolidated with acceptable standards after extensive debates on the criteria for excluding articles, with all coefficients above 0.8 in the third round of comments.

In the third round, 90 articles are selected for the study. However, the fourth review is necessary, as highlighted in the waterfall diagram.

By reviewing the references from the articles selected for the study, it became clear that there was a need to include the article by Huang and Liu (2005) which appears as a reference in the article by Singh et al. (2011) and which did not appear as a result of the search in the databases.

As a result, 91 articles were selected for the study with a satisfactory coefficient of 0.899. It can be seen that most of the abstracts chosen, as detailed in Figure 2, refer to the EBSCO and EMERALD databases, with 38% and 31% respectively.

Hά a reasonable assumption about the quality of the studies selected, since all the selection was carried out through peer review.

However, when comparing the search results with the selected articles, there is a high dispersion in the EBSCO database, which justifies the large number of articles from commercial magazines and advertising or articles based on the author's opinion.

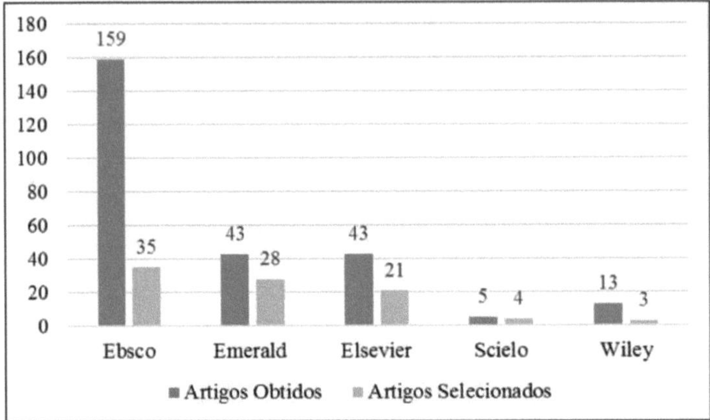

Figure 2 - Comparison between the number of articles obtained in the search and the number of articles selected.

Source: Prepared by the author.

After selecting the articles for the study, the papers were read in full to analyze and summarize the approaches taken by the authors.

All the information regarding the articles is collected and detailed in a file, where the data is later interpreted and results are generated. The types of information collected in the articles selected for the study are located in Topic 7.2. Appendix B.

3. Descriptive analysis

3.1. Study identification

The 91 articles selected for study are listed in Table 2, together with the year of research, the number of citations obtained from the *ISI Web of Knowledge*, the average number of annual citations obtained from the *ISI Web of Knowledge* and the name of the journal.

Table 2 - Summary of article results.

References	No. of Quotes	Average citations	Source*
Hines & Rich (1997)	105	5,83	IJOPM
Hines et al. (1998)	0	0,00	IJLM
Hines et al. (1999)	0	0,00	BIJ
Sullivan et al. (2002)	31	2,38	RCIM
Lima & Zawslak (2003)	1	0,08	GP
Roldan & Miyake (2004)	1	0,09	GP
Holweg (2005)	47	4,7	IJOPM
Huang & Liu (2005)	8	0,80	IJPR
Kaale et al. (2005)	1	1,00	AEM
Kocakulah & Upson (2005)	0	0,00	RHFM
Braglia et al. (2006)	36	0,00	IJPR
Lummus et al. (2006)	0	0,00	TQM
Singh et al. (2006)	18	2,00	IJPR
Abdulmalek & Rajgopal (2007)	102	12,75	IJPE
Adrian et al. (2007)	0	0,00	BMPJ
Lawrence et al. (2007)	0	0,00	EIDI
Lian & Van Landeghem (2007)	24	3,00	IJPR
Barber & Tietje (2008)	0	0,00	JPSSM
Bevilacqua et al. (2008)	1	0,14	PMJ
Lasa et al. (2008)	0	0,00	BPMJ
Matt (2008)	0	0,00	JMTM
Serrano et al. (2008)	19	2,71	IJPR
Seth et al. (2008)	0	0,00	JMTM
Alvarez et al. (2009)	16	2,67	IJAMT
Salgado et al. (2009)	1	0,17	GP
Singh & Sharma (2009)	0	0,00	MBEs

AA - Assembly Automation; AC - Built Environment; AEM - Academic Emergency Medicine; AJHSP - American Journal of Heath-System Pharmacy; APLM - Arch Pathol Lab Med; BIJ - Benchmarking: An International Journal; BMJ QS - BMJ Quality & Safety; BPMJ - Business Process Management Journal; CIE - Computers & Industrial Engineering; CIRP JMST - CIRP Journal of Manufacturing Science and Technology ; CJEM - Canadian Journal of Emergency Medicine; DAAAM ISB - DAAAM International Scientific Book; DDT - Drug Discovery Today; EIDI - Electronic and Industrial Distribution Industries; EJR - European Journal of Radiology; ESWA - Expert Systems with Applications; FPJ - Forest Products Journal; GP - Gestao e Produçâo; IJAMT - International Journal Advanced Manufacturing Technology; IJCIM - International Journal of Computer Integrated Manufacturing; IJCL - The International Journal of Clinical Leadership; IJLM - The International Journal of Logistics Management; IJLSS - International Journal of Lean Six Sigma; IJOPM - International Journal of Operations & Production Management; IJPE - International Journal of Production Economics; IJPR - International Journal of Production Research; IJQRM - International Journal of Quality & Reliability Management; JACS - Journal of the American College of Surgeons; JAMR - Journal of Advances in Management Research; JAS - Journal of Applied Sciences; JCEM - Journal of Construction Engineering and Management; JCP - Journal of Cleaner Production; JEDT - Journal of Engineering, Design and Technology; JME - Journal of Management In Engineering; JMSY - Journal of Manufacturing Systems; JMTM - Journal of Manufacturing Technology Management; JPSSM - Journal of Personal Selling & Sales Management; JSEP - Journal of Software: Evolution and Process; LAS - Langenbecks Arch Surg; LHS - Leadership in Health Services, MBEs - Measuring Business Excellence, PE - Procedia Engineering; PJSS - Pakistan Journal of Social Sciences; PMJ - Project Management Journal; PROCIR - Procedia CIRP; Prod - Production; PT - Procedia Technology; QE - Quality Engineering; QSHC - Quality Safety Health Care; RCIM - Robotics and Computer- Integrated Manufacturing; RHFM - Research in Healthcare Financial Management; SCMIJ - Supply Chain Management: An International Journal; TOURMAN - Tourism Management; TQM - Total Quality Management

Number of citations obtained on November 17, 2014.

Updated on February 15, 2015.

Table 2 - Summary of article results.

References	No. of citations	Average citations	Source*
Wang et al. (2009)	7	1,17	JCEM
Wee & Wu (2009)	19	3,17	SCMIJ
Yu et al. (2009)	7	1,17	JCEM
Al-Tahat (2010)	0	0,00	JAS
Chen et al. (2010)	13	2,60	IJPR
Grove et al. (2010)	2	0,40	QSHC
L'Hommedieu & Kappeler (2010)	2	0,40	AJHSP
Ng et al.(2010)	26	5,20	CJEM
Singh et al. (2010)	0	0,00	IJLSS

Vinodh et al. (2010)	0	0,00	JMTM
Cima et al. (2011)	22	5,50	JACS
Cookson et al. (2011)	0	0,00	IJCL
Garrett & Lee (2011)	2	0,50	EQ
Gurumurthy & Kodali (2011)	0	0,00	JMTM
Kuhlang et al. (2011)	0	0,00	CIRP JMST
Lu et al. (2011)	9	2,25	IJCIM
Nepal, et al. (2011)	0	0,00	JMTM
Schwarz et al. 2011)	0	0,00	LAS
Singh et al. (2011)	8	2,00	IJAMT
Wang et al. (2011)	0	0,00	FPJ
Yang & Lu (2011)	8	2,00	IJPR
Agyapong-Koduaa et al. (2012)	1	0,33	IJPR
Carter et al. (2012)	4	1,33	AEM
Chen et al. (2012)	2	0,67	AA
Chiarini (2012)	0	0,00	LHS
Duranik, et al. (2012)	0	0,00	DAAAM ISB
Garg & Naido (2012)	0	0,00	PJSS
Gibbons et al. (2012)	0	0,00	IJLSS
Hofacker et al. (2012)	0	0,00	AC
Jiménez et al. (2012)	6	2,00	IJPR
Hydes et al. (2012)	4	1,33	BMJ
Rahani & Al-Ashraf (2012)	0	0,00	PE
Teichgraber & de Bucourt (2012)	4	1,33	EJR

AA - Assembly Automation; AC - Built Environment; AEM - Academic Emergency Medicine; AJHSP - American Journal of Heath-System Pharmacy; APLM - Arch Pathol Lab Med; BIJ - Benchmarking: An International Journal; BMJ QS - BMJ Quality & Safety; BPMJ - Business Process Management Journal; CIE - Computers & Industrial Engineering; CIRP JMST - CIRP Journal of Manufacturing Science and Technology ; CJEM - Canadian Journal of Emergency Medicine; DAAAM ISB - DAAAM International Scientific Book; DDT - Drug Discovery Today; EIDI - Electronic and Industrial Distribution Industries; EJR - European Journal of Radiology; ESWA - Expert Systems with Applications; FPJ - Forest Products Journal; GP - Gestao e Produçâo; IJAMT - International Journal Advanced Manufacturing Technology; IJCIM - International Journal of Computer Integrated Manufacturing; IJCL - The International Journal of Clinical Leadership; IJLM - The International Journal of Logistics Management; IJLSS - International Journal of Lean Six Sigma; IJOPM - International Journal of Operations & Production Management; IJPE - International Journal of Production Economics; IJPR - International Journal of Production Research; IJQRM - International Journal of Quality & Reliability Management; JACS - Journal of the American College of Surgeons; JAMR - Journal of Advances in Management Research; JAS - Journal of Applied Sciences; JCEM - Journal of Construction Engineering and Management; JCP - Journal of Cleaner Production; JEDT -

Journal of Engineering, Design and Technology; JME - Journal of Management In Engineering; JMSY - Journal of Manufacturing Systems; JMTM - Journal of Manufacturing Technology Management; JPSSM - Journal of Personal Selling & Sales Management; JSEP - Journal of Software: Evolution and Process; LAS - Langenbecks Arch Surg; LHS - Leadership in Health Services, MBEs - Measuring Business Excellence, PE - Procedia Engineering; PJSS - Pakistan Journal of Social Sciences; PMJ - Project Management Journal; PROCIR - Procedia CIRP; Prod - Production; PT - Procedia Technology; QE - Quality Engineering; QSHC - Quality Safety Health Care; RCIM - Robotics and Computer-Integrated Manufacturing; RHFM - Research in Healthcare Financial Management; SCMIJ - Supply Chain Management: An International Journal; TOURMAN - Tourism Management; TQM - Total Quality Management

Number of citations obtained on November 17, 2014.

Updated on February 15, 2015.

Table 2 - Summary of article results.

References	No. of citations	Average citations	Source*
Wong et al. (2012)	0	0,00	APLM
Xie & Peng (2012)	0	0,00	BMJ
Chen et al. (2013)	0	4,00	IJAMT
Chen et al. (2013)	8	4,00	ESWA
Chiarini (2013)	0	0,00	LHS
Folinas et al. (2013)	0	0,00	EN
Marques et al. (2013)	0	0,00	PROCIR
Matt et al. (2013)	0	0,00	PROCIR
Singh & Singh (2013)	0	0,00	JAMR
Souza et al. (2013)	0	0,00	IJQRM
Tabanli & Ertay (2013)	1	0,50	IJAMT
Tanco et al. (2013)	1	0,50	IJAMT
Vinodh et al. (2013)	0	0,00	JDET
Vlachos & Bogdanovic (2013)	2	2,00	TOURMAN
Yu et al. (2013)	2	1,00	JME
Abdelhadi & Shakoor (2014)	0	0,00	LHS
Basu & Dan (2014)	0	0,00	IJLSS
Bauer et al. (2014)	0	0,00	PROCIR
Brown et al. (2014)	0	0,00	JCP
Cevikcan & Durmusoglu (2014)	0	0,00	CIE
Chiarini (2014)	0	0,00	JCP
Faulkner & Badurdeen (2014)	0	0,00	JCP
Haefner et al. (2014)	1	1,00	PROCIR
Heinzen et al. (2014)	0	0,00	DDT

Jasti & Sharma (2014)	0	0,00	IJLSS
Khurum et al. (2014)	0	0,00	JSEP
Librelato et al. (2014)	0	0,00	BPMJ
Matt (2014)	0	0,00	JMTM
Müller et al. (2014)	0	0,00	PROCIR
Prashar (2014)	0	0,00	TQMJ
Tyagi et al. (2014)	0	0,00	IJPE
Susilawati et al. (2015)	0	0,00	JMSY

AA - Assembly Automation; AC - Built Environment; AEM - Academic Emergency Medicine; AJHSP - American Journal of Heath-System Pharmacy; APLM - Arch Pathol Lab Med; BIJ - Benchmarking: An International Journal; BMJ QS - BMJ Quality & Safety; BPMJ - Business Process Management Journal; CIE - Computers & Industrial Engineering; CIRP JMST - CIRP Journal of Manufacturing Science and Technology ; CJEM - Canadian Journal of Emergency Medicine; DAAAM ISB - DAAAM International Scientific Book; DDT - Drug Discovery Today; EIDI - Electronic and Industrial Distribution Industries; EJR - European Journal of Radiology; ESWA - Expert Systems with Applications; FPJ - Forest Products Journal; GP - Gestao e Produçâo; IJAMT - International Journal Advanced Manufacturing Technology; IJCIM - International Journal of Computer Integrated Manufacturing; IJCL - The International Journal of Clinical Leadership; IJLM - The International Journal of Logistics Management; IJLSS - International Journal of Lean Six Sigma; IJOPM - International Journal of Operations & Production Management; IJPE - International Journal of Production Economics; IJPR - International Journal of Production Research; IJQRM - International Journal of Quality & Reliability Management; JACS - Journal of the American College of Surgeons; JAMR - Journal of Advances in Management Research; JAS - Journal of Applied Sciences; JCEM - Journal of Construction Engineering and Management; JCP - Journal of Cleaner Production; JEDT - Journal of Engineering, Design and Technology; JME - Journal of Management In Engineering; JMSY - Journal of Manufacturing Systems; JMTM - Journal of Manufacturing Technology Management; JPSSM - Journal of Personal Selling & Sales Management; JSEP - Journal of Software: Evolution and Process; LAS - Langenbecks Arch Surg; LHS - Leadership in Health Services, MBEs - Measuring Business Excellence, PE - Procedia Engineering; PJSS - Pakistan Journal of Social Sciences; PMJ - Project Management Journal; PROCIR - Procedia CIRP; Prod - Production; PT - Procedia Technology; QE - Quality Engineering; QSHC - Quality Safety Health Care; RCIM - Robotics and Computer- Integrated Manufacturing; RHFM - Research in Healthcare Financial Management; SCMIJ - Supply Chain Management: An International Journal; TOURMAN - Tourism Management; TQM - Total Quality Management

Number of citations obtained on November 17, 2014.

Updated February 15, 2015

As shown in Table 2, only one author has published more than three studies on the subject (Chen et al. 2010; Chen et al. 2012; Chen et al. 2013; Chen et al. 2013). Interest in the subject is growing, as evidenced by the articles published in recent years, shown in Figure 3.

Publications on the VSM are frequent, with the first appearing in

1997 and more concentrated from 2011 onwards (Figure 3). It is important to note that from 1997 to 2011, 47 articles were published, while Singh et al. (2011) looked at 49 texts. The systematic review by Singh et al. (2011) includes studies of the VSM based on books such as Womack et al. (1999) and

Womack and Jones (1996), unlike this research, which takes an article-based approach.

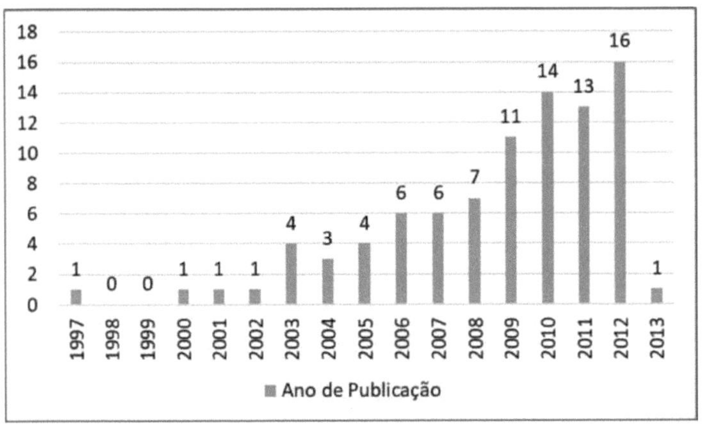

Figure 3 - Number of documents retrieved for the systematic review analysis. Source: Prepared by the author.

The second and third columns of Table 2 represent, respectively, the number of citations for each article and the average number of citations per year obtained from the *ISI Web of Knowledge*. The *ISI Web of Knowledge* platform was chosen for four main reasons (Thomé et al., 2012a), similar to Google Scholar (GS): *(i) it* is freely available on the Internet; *(ii) it* is supposedly fast; *(iii) it* includes grey scientific literature (documentation produced by ministries, government agencies, private organizations, NGOs, cultural and academic institutions and that generated at meetings and congresses); and *(iv) it* compares citation indices.

In total, 37% of the citations are concentrated in two authors (Hines & Rich 1997; Abdulmalek & Rajgopal 2007), whose publications are not recent but are of great relevance. In particular, one article describes ways of applying the VSM purely or in combination with other tools and allows the researcher to choose the method best suited to their reality (Hines & Rich, 1997), while Abdulmalek & Rajgopal (2007) describe the benefits obtained by using the VSM to reduce production *lead times* and in-process inventory in a steel industry. Both have the highest average number of citations per year.

The fourth column describes the origin of the publications, most of which are concentrated in journals focusing on research in the production and manufacturing areas. The largest number of papers appeared in IJPR (10% of publications), followed by JMTM (7% of publications) and IJAMT (5% of publications).

3.2. VSM description

VSM (*Value Stream Mapping*), introduced by Rother & Shook (1998), is a relatively simple value stream mapping method (using paper and pencils) with a procedure for constructing manufacturing scenarios (Vieira, 2006). This mapping takes into account both the flow of materials and the flow of information and helps greatly in the process of visualizing the current situation and constructing the future situation (Vieira, 2006).

Mapping is encouraged to be done with paper and pencils, although software already exists for this (Vieira, 2006). The reason for this is to encourage users of the tool to walk through the value stream (Pojasek, 2004).

On the other hand, the VSM is a tool that, like other lean production tools, focuses more on issues related to reducing the *lead time* (time dimension) of systems (Vieira, 2006). The time dimension seems to be the main and sometimes only dimension considered in this type of tool (Vieira, 2006).

The VSM is a continuous improvement tool that creates a virtuous circle in which, after carrying out the actions to achieve the future state map, the future state map becomes the present state map and new improvement actions are carried out to achieve the new future state map (Vieira, 2006). This cycle usually takes between three and six months (Rother & Shook, 1998).

The value stream runs perpendicular to the process stations, the same as Shingo (1996a) stated when he said that the process (value stream) runs perpendicular to the operations (process stations) (Vieira, 2006). The value stream map helps to focus improvement efforts on the stream and not on the processes (Vieira, 2006).

For Rother and Shook (1998) *kaizen* can be divided into two types: process kaizen and flow kaizen. Flow kaizen would be more linked to management because of its interdepartmental nature and because it is making improvements to the flow of value. Process *kaizen* would be more linked to the shop floor because it deals with specific issues in the process, which may not have a major impact on the value stream, but can significantly improve operating conditions. VSM is used to improve internal processes ("door-to-door" mapping), but it is used to map the entire supply chain because the logic of reducing *lead time,* through continuous improvement, to gain efficiency and quality in the value stream is the same (Gardner & Cooper, 2003).

Door-to-door mapping means mapping from the warehouse door to the finished goods dispatch door (Vieira, 2006). In general, the mapping tool, as presented by Vieira (2006) has the following characteristics: *(i)* provide a common, visual and symbolic language; *(ii)* be easy to visualize and understand by the lowest hierarchical level that will use it; *(iii)* help to see the flow of value through departments and processes; *(iv)* show the relationship between the flow of information and the flow of materials in the manufacturing system; *(v)* support the improvement of the system as a whole and not just one of its parts; (*vi)* help identify the sources of waste; *(vii)* add lean manufacturing techniques and concepts and; *(viii)* form the basis of an implementation plan.

3.3. Type of study

The research covers the type of study classified into seven categories, as shown in Table 3: *(i)* case study; (*ii)* research study - *survey*; (*iii)* mathematical model; (*iv)* action research; (*v)* simulation; (*vi)* literature review and; *(vii)* multi-method.

The choice of these methodologies is justified by the fact that, according to Filippini (1997), Berto and Nakano (2000) and Miguel (2007), these approaches are the most widely used in research related to production and operations management. The definition of each type of study used in the research can be found in Appendix A under Topic 7.1. The methodological approach used in the articles was more concentrated in case studies, with 63% of the publications, as shown in Figure 4.

The prevalence of case study research on the VSM is consistent (Jasti & Sharma, 2014). Both the *survey* study method and the simulation model account for 12% and 14% of the articles respectively.

For the action research method, no research was identified and for the mathematical model, two publications were identified.

Eight articles used the multi-method approach, where Gurumurthy & Kodali, (2011) and Vinodh et al. (2013) apply both case study and simulation. Tabanli & Ertay (2013) apply both case study and action research. Susilawati et al. (2015) apply both *survey* and mathematical model.

Huang & Liu (2005), Lian & Van Landeghem (2007) and Xie & Peng (2012) apply both the mathematical model and the simulation and, finally, Singh et al. (2011) apply both the literature review and the case study.

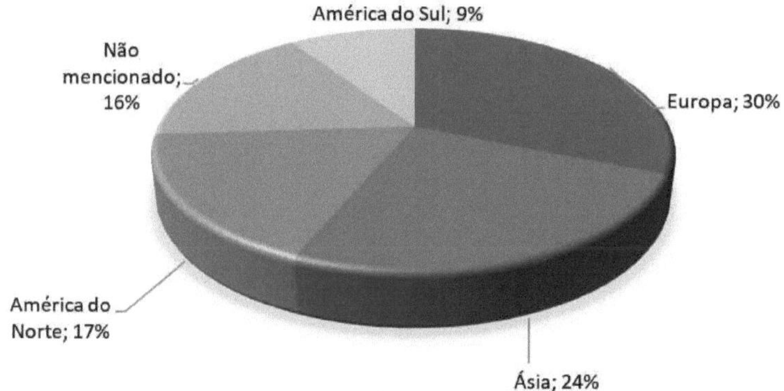

Figure 4 - Percentage of methodological approach used in VSM publications.

Source: Prepared by the author.

Table 3 - Description of the selected publications by methodology used.

Methodology used	Selected articles
Case studies	Hines et al. (1999), Lima & Zawslak (2003), Kaale et al. (2005), Kocakulah & Upson (2005), Braglia et al. (2006), Lummus et al. (2006), Adrian et al. (2007), Lawrence et al. (2007), Barber & Tietje (2008), Bevilacqua et al. (2008), Lasa et al. (2008), Serrano et al. (2008), Alvarez et al. (2009), Singh & Sharma (2009), Yu et al. (2009), Wee & Wu (2009), Al-Tahat (2010), Chen et al. (2010), L'Hommedieu & Kappeler (2010), Ng et al. (2010), Singh, et al. (2010), Vinodh et al. (2010), Cima et al. (2011), Cookson et al. (2011), Garrett & Lee (2011), Kuhlang et al. (2011), Nepal et al. (2011), Schwarz et al. (2011), Wang et al. (2011), Agyapong-Koduaa et al. (2012), Carter et al. (2012), Chiarini (2012), Duranik et al. (2012), Garg & Naido (2012), Hofacker et al. (2012), Hydes et al. (2012), Rahani & Al-Ashraf (2012), Wong et al. (2012), Chen et al. (2013), Chen et al. (2013), Chiarini (2013), Marques et al. (2013), Matt et al. (2013), Singh & Singh (2013), Souza et al. (2013), Tanco et al. (2013), Yu et al. (2013), Bauer et al. (2014), Brown et al. (2014), Chiarini (2014), Faulkner & Badurdeen (2014), Haefner et al. (2014), Jasti & Sharma (2014), Khurum et al. (2014), Librelato et al. (2014), Matt (2014), Prashar (2014).
Research study - *survey*	Hines & Rich (1997), Hines et al. (1998), Roldan & Miyake (2004), Holweg (2005), Matt (2008), Seth et al. (2008), Gibbons et al. (2012), Jiménez et al. (2012), Vlachos & Bogdanovic (2013), Abdelhadi & Shakoor (2014), Basu & Dan (2014).
Mathematical model	Singh et al. (2006), Cevikcan & Durmusoglu (2014).
Simulation	Sullivan et al. (2002), Abdulmaleka & Rajgopal (2007), Salgado et al. (2009), Wang et al. (2009), Grove et al. (2010), Lu et al. (2011), Yang & Lu, (2011), Chen et al. (2012), Teichgraber & de Bucourt (2012), Folinas et al. (2013), Heinzen et al. (2014), Müller et al. (2014), Tyagi et al. (2014).
Multi-method	Case Study/Simulation - Gurumurthy & Kodali, (2011), Vinodh et al. (2013). Case Study/Action Research - Tabanli & Ertay (2013). *Survey* Research Study/Mathematical Model - Susilawati et al. (2015). Mathematical Model/Simulation - Huang & Liu (2005), Lian & Van Landeghem (2007); Xie & Peng (2012). Literature Review/Case Study - Singh et al. (2011).

Source: Prepared by the author.

4. Results and discussion

The results will be presented in two categories: a *framework* summarizing the literature review and a description of the study.

4.1. Summary of the literature review - *framework*

The conceptual framework presented in Figure 5 aims to organize the literature review on the subject. It is based on a framework originating from previous research (Thomé et al. 2012a; Bhamu & Sangwan 2014; Thome et al. 2014) and on an exploratory analysis of the VSM articles selected for study in this research based on Cooper's methodology (2010). The structure of the framework covers all the elements needed to describe the application of VSM, such as: *(i)* business objectives and goals; *(ii)* the context; *(iii)* motivation; *(iv)* implementation; *(v)* output and; *(vi)* results.

In simplified form, the structure was adopted based on the elements of the VSM implementation process.

Business objectives and goals must be related to the company's strategy and their deployment must be carried out at the other organizational levels (Thomé et al., 2014).

In the organizational context, the type of industry, economic context, country and local culture must be considered (Thomé et al., 2014). The economic sector involved and the type of production system studied should also be taken into account (Thomé et al., 2014).

The motivation for applying the VSM refers to the problems researched in the literature.

Implementation is the set of organized efforts to achieve the goals and objectives, considering the context of the VSM, which involves *(i)* setting objectives; *(ii)* identifying losses; *(iii)* planning and executing *kaizens and*; *(iv)* analyzing *kaizens*, generating the current value stream map and the future value stream map as products.

The output and results elaborated in the *framework* consider the output variables after implementing the VSM, as well as organizational results such as profit, customer satisfaction, *market share* and the environment.

The theoretical framework has therefore been organized around the main elements for identifying opportunities to eliminate waste, the systematic classification of which is described in the following topics.

Figure 5 - Summary of the literature review on VSM.

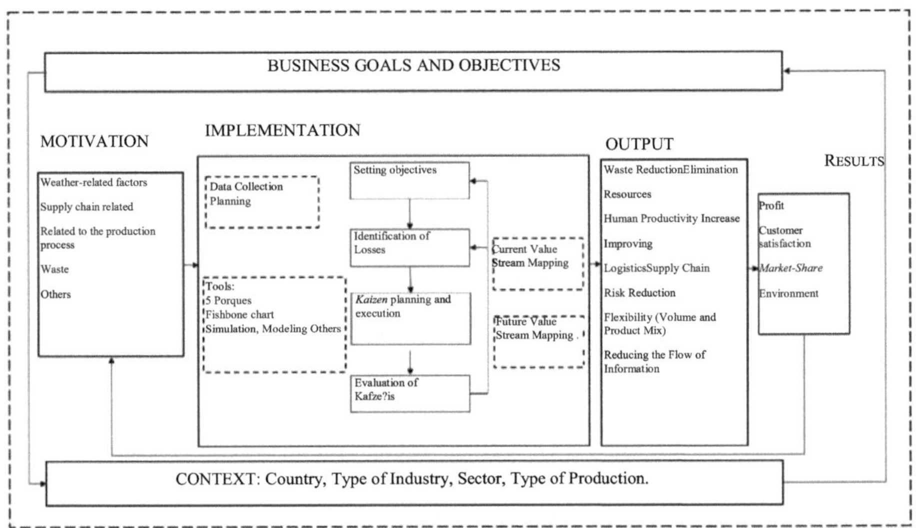

Source: Prepared by the author.

4.2. Study description

The following sections present a literature review organized according to the *framework* structure proposed for the research.

4.2.1. Business objectives and goals

Some companies report huge benefits from using VSM, while many industries do not get the desired results (Mohanty et al., 2007; Lasa et al. 2008, Bhamu & Sangwan, 2014).

One of the reasons for this is the tool's lack of alignment with the company's corporate strategy (Salgado et al., 2009).

One of the most important tasks of top management is to define strategy and ensure that it is rolled out to all levels of the organization (Ferro et al., 2010).

The deployment of the strategy is connected to the company's basic values and premises, in particular the prevailing leadership style (Ferro, et al., 2010). Any change in the production system aimed at implementing a lean model requires clear direction, with a clear vision of the goals to be achieved. Otherwise, it is very difficult to successfully adopt the fundamental principles of lean production in a company (Mohanty et al., 2007; Lasa et al. 2008).

In the process of implementing the VSM, it is important to emphasize efforts in the value streams that require substantial improvement from a broad perspective, with the business objective at its core (Liker & Convis, 2013). Improvement targets should be set for the chosen product families, i.e. setting qualitative objectives that can later be quantified (Ferro, 2005), as in the case of reducing costs by reducing rework (Singh et al., 2006; Tabanli & Ertay, 2013; Bauer et al., 2014), gaining physical space to enable implementation (Matt, 2008; Jiménez et al., 2012; Bauer et al., 2014; Prashar, 2014) or reducing *lead time* to increase responsiveness to market changes (Hines & Rich, 1997; Hines et al., 1999; Kaale et al., 2005; Abdulmalek & Rajgopal, 2007; Lawrence et al.., 2007; Lian & Van Landeghem, 2007; Barber & Tietje, 2008; Bevilacqua et al., 2008; Lasa et al., 2008; Serrano et al., 2008; Seth et al., 2008; Wang et al., 2009; Yu et al., 2009; L'Hommedieu & Kappeler, 2010; Vinodh et al., 2010; Garrett & Lee, 2011; Kuhlang et al., 2011; Nepal et al., 2011; Duranik et al.., 2012; Jiménez et al., 2012; Rahani & al-Ashraf, 2012; Wong et al., 2012; Chen et al., 2013; Tanco et al., 2013; Vinodh et al., 2013; Abdelhadi & Shakoor, 2014; Brown et al.., 2014; Cevikcan & Durmusoglu, 2014; Faulkner & Badurdeen, 2014; Heinzen et al., 2014; Librelato et al., 2014; Müller et al., 2014; Tyagi et al., 2014).

Everyone must be aware of the objectives and decisions to be made (Bhamu & Sangwan, 2014). Goals, objectives and actions must be interlinked down to the operational level (Hines & Rich, 1997).

The effective operation of the *Lean* philosophy requires clear communication, not only between operational units, but also between all segments of the value chain (Storch & Lim, 1999). Every organization needs a vision together with objectives (Liker & Convis, 2013).

Waste is caused by poorly defined objectives and targets and undeclared or uninformed responsibilities (Salgado et al., 2009). Meetings should be held so that the objectives can be presented to the respective areas responsible and then more specific action plans can be drawn up (Liker & Convis, 2013).

Objectives should be discussed and planned as the goals set by top management spread throughout the organization and are transformed into more specific, actionable plans (Liker & Convis, 2013). The unit as a whole must work to ensure that all levels of the organization (HR, sales, *marketing*, finance, operations/production) are clear about their metrics and goals to be achieved (Liker & Convis, 2013). The involvement of the members boosts confidence to face the challenges throughout the application of the tool and reinforces the capacity for teamwork, providing opportunities to show leadership skills and solve problems with logic (Bhamu & Sangwan, 2014).

When the use of the tool is not aligned with the company's corporate strategy and does not meet the needs of the supply chain, the mapping is carried out based on the operational objective of just one business unit (Salgado et al., 2009) or different departments work on disconnected projects, it is likely that the company will not obtain great benefits (Liker & Convis, 2013).

However, breaking down high-level business goals into more specific goals for each department, with well-designed action plans and intensive kaizen, will allow these separate efforts to realize significant results for the core business (Liker & Convis, 2013).

Thus, the deployment of the strategy, aligned with the implementation of the tool, guarantees the involvement of everyone aimed at meeting the objectives and targets with a focus on the macro needs of the business. It must be part of the management system, both to help the company grow consistently and to deal with crises without having to resort to counterproductive measures in the long term (Ferro, 2005).

4.2.2. Context

The relationship between the implementation of lean production and organizational culture can be very sensitive depending on the context.

Issues such as different countries with different customs, different workloads, different degrees of development and different types of industries must be considered when using lean production (Bhamu & Sangwan, 2014).

Research on VSM is carried out in countries on the European continent (Italy, Germany, United Kingdom, Spain, Austria, Belgium, England, Greece, Portugal and Switzerland), Asia (India, China, Indonesia, Jordan, Malaysia, Turkey), North America (United States and Canada), South America (Brazil, Spain, Argentina and Peru), the Middle East (Saudi Arabia) and the African continent (South Africa). European countries (mainly Italy and Germany) have the highest number of publications (27 cases), followed by Asia (mainly India) with 22 publications.

The result indicates that many organizations, both in India and in other countries, are implementing the principles and concepts of Lean Production in order to achieve a competitive advantage over other organizations (Gurumurthy & Kodali, 2011). North America followed with fifteen publications, South America with eight and Africa and the Middle East with two publications each.

Fifteen publications did not mention where the study was carried out (Hines & Rich, 1997; Hines et al., 1998; Hines et al., 1999; Holweg, 2005; Adrian et al., 2007; Barber & Tietje, 2008; Yu et al, 2009; Garrett & Lee, 2011; Chen et al., 2012; Duranik et al., 2012; Teichgraber & de Bucourt, 2012; Xie & Peng, 2012; Chen et al., 2013; Folinas et al., 2013; Faulkner & Badurdeen, 2014).

The distribution by geographical region is shown in Figure 6.

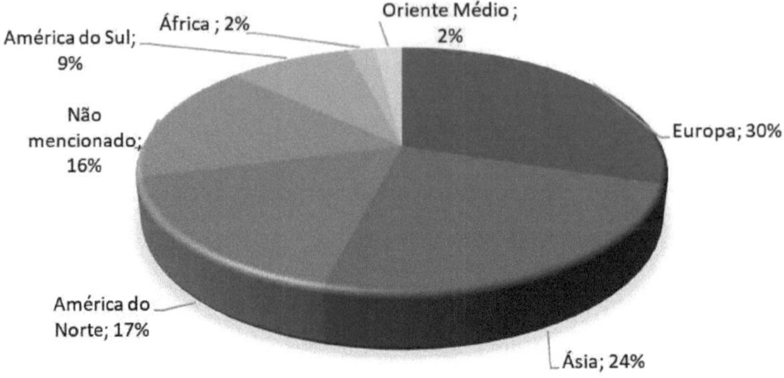

Figure 6 - Percentage of publications by geographical region.

Source: Prepared by the author.

It is clear that VSM publications began in European countries in 2006. Publications in North America began in 2002 and became more frequent in 2005, while publications in Asia began in 2005 and became more concentrated in 2011.

The VSM appears systematically as a tool to help analyze and improve industrial processes (Braglia et al., 2006). However, the application of VSM is not restricted to linear processes or factory floor environments (Braglia et al., 2006).

When it comes to the type of industry, hospitals and clinics appear frequently, followed by the automotive industry. Two publications do not mention the type of industry (Duranik et al., 2012; Basu & Dan, 2014) and two present the application through a hypothetical example (Sullivan et al., 2002; Chen et al., 2012). The type of industry in which the VSM study was applied, as well as the frequency in which they appear, are shown in Table 4.

Table 4 - Description of the type of industry and its frequency

Type of industry	Frequency	Frequency (%)
Hospitals and Clinics	17	17%
Automotive industry	14	14%
Metal-Mechanical Industry	7	7%
Electronics industry	6	6%
Construction	4	4%

Distributor	4	4%
Steel industry	4	4%
Railroad Industry	3	3%
Supermarket	3	3%
Food Industry	2	2%
Domestic Appliances Industry	3	3%
Metal Engineering Industry	2	2%
Furniture Industry	3	3%
Plastics industry	2	2%
Telecommunications Company	1	1%
Electrical Wire Manufacturer	1	1%
Shower Cabin Manufacturer	1	1%
Electric Detonator Industry	1	1%
Business Strategy and *Supply Chain*	1	1%
Agri-food industry	1	1%
Heating Industry	1	1%
Aviation industry	1	1%
Beverage Industry	1	1%
Oil Distribution Block Industry	1	1%
Construction Industry	1	1%
Printing Industry	1	1%
Wood Industry	1	1%
Machinery Industry	1	1%
Medicines Industry	1	1%
Assembly industry	1	1%
Edible Cottonseed Oil Industry	1	1%
Oil industry	1	1%
Bath Products Industry	1	1%
Office Products and Stationery Industry	1	1%
Sanitation and Bathroom Industry	1	1%
Tourism	1	1%
Not Mentioned/Hypothetical Example	4	4%
Grand total	**101**	**100%**

Source: Author's responsibility.

The types of sectors in which the methods have been applied are very diverse, encompassing industry/manufacturing, healthcare, construction, distribution, supermarkets, logistics and supply chain, aviation, energy, tourism and telecommunications.

VSM applications by economic sector are still mostly concentrated in manufacturing with 52 publications, where the practice originated.

However, there is a significant amount of research done in the health care sector (17 cases), where five publications are related to the private sector (Kaale et al., 2005; Kocakulah & Upson, 2005; Ng et al., 2010; Schwarz et al., 2011; Wong et al., 2012), 10 publications to the public sector (Lummus et al., 2006; Grove et al., 2010; L'Hommedieu & Kappeler, 2010; Cima et al., 2011; Carter et al., 2012; Chiarini, 2012; Hydes et al., 2012; Teichgraber & de Bucourt, 2012, Chiarini, 2013; Abdelhadi & Shakoor, 2014) and two publications where the body was not mentioned (Cookson et al., 2011; Xie & Peng, 2012). Figure 7 describes the number of publications by type of sector.

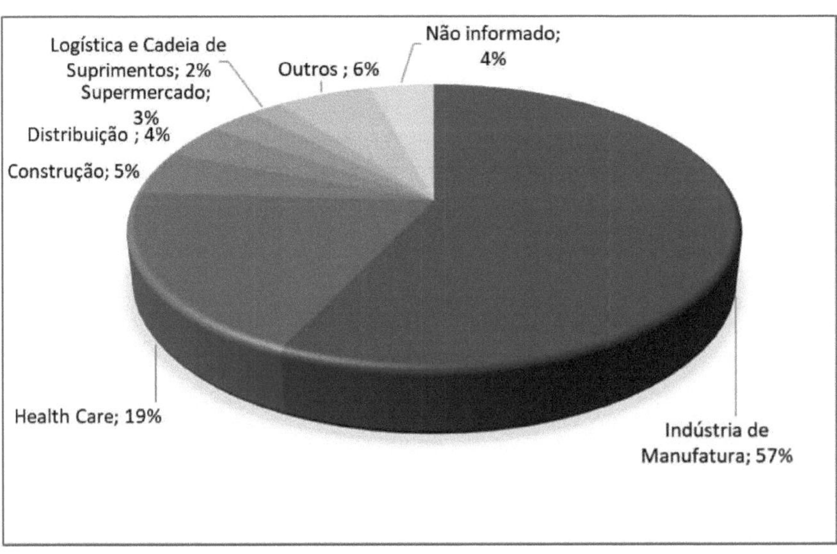

Figure 7 - Percentage of publications by type of sector.

Source: Author's responsibility.

As shown in Figure 8, VSM publications in the manufacturing sector are frequent, starting in 2003. In the *Health Care sector*, publications began in 2005, with a large concentration in 2012.

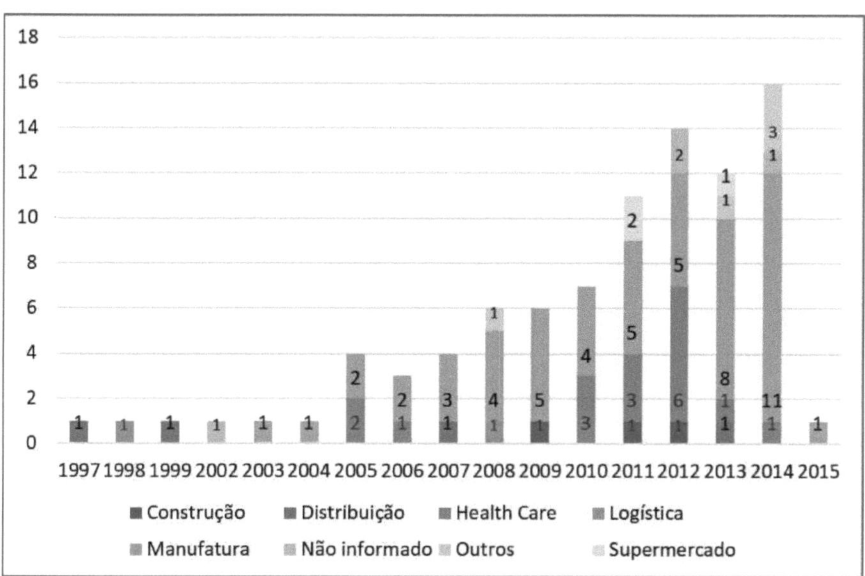

Figure 8 - Percentage of publications by year and type of sector. Source: Prepared by the author.

Production systems can be classified according to the type of production strategy: *(i)* push and *(ii)* pull.

Pushed production corresponds to anticipating future demand in time, based on schedules made on the basis of sales forecasts (Bowersox & Closs, 1979). Pushed production is the type of production that has been implemented the most in industries (Corrêa & Gianesi, 1994).

On the other hand, pull production is characterized by the progressive elimination of waste, by continuous flow, by production according to customer demand at the time and in the quantity set by the customer and, finally, by a close relationship and partnership with suppliers (Lima & Zawslak, 2003).

Based on the research carried out, it can be seen that both the pull and push production systems have well-distributed results (Figure 9), with 42 and 43 publications respectively. Five cases did not mention the type of production (Hines et al., 1998; Sullivan et al., 2002; Chen et al., 2012; Duranik et al., 2012; Basu & Dan, 2014), while one study (Lima & Zawislak, 2003) describes the implementation of the VSM in five companies in the automotive sector, where two companies work with a made-to-order parts system and the others work with a sales forecasting system and use safety stock as a strategy.

Figure 9 - Percentage of publications by type of production.

Source: Prepared by the author.

4.2.3. Motivation

The motivations reflect the problems addressed by the authors in the companies surveyed. The literature shows that these motivations for applying the VSM in the sectors (industry/manufacturing, *healthcare*, construction, distribution, supermarket, logistics/supply chain and others) basically follow the same guidelines. The categories of motivators and the authors' descriptions are shown in Table 5. The elimination of losses is the main driver, followed by time-related factors (high *lead times* and high cycle times).

When looking exclusively at factors related to losses, according to Antunes (2008) and Bornia (2002), losses are conceptualized as unnecessary operations or movements that generate costs and do not add value and, therefore, should be eliminated from the system.

Maintaining high inventories, for example, is wasteful, as it does not add value to the product and requires expenditure (Bornia, 2002). In the case of industries, Lima & Zawislak (2003) describe that using a considerable part of the production area to stock finished products is considered wasteful. This is due to the fact that the company works at a pushed production pace in relation to its lower output products. Reducing stock in process and finished product stock is also a concern for Tanco et al. (2013). One possible reason for the existence of such high stock levels is the culture of safety stocks as a buffer against sales fluctuations and a deficiency in production scheduling (Lima & Zawislak 2003).

In *health care*, Teichgraber & Bucourt (2012) describe the high stock levels of endovascular prostheses. Excess stock can prevent deficiencies from being identified, such as delays in deliveries, as well as complaints from managers about the capital tied up, which can lead to a lack of resources in other areas (Teichgraber & Bucourt, 2012). Losses related to waiting and transportation are also very common.

Cases such as high queue waiting times (Hydes et al., 2012) and high waiting times for administrative activities (Roldan & Miyake, 2004; Chen et al., 2013; Tanco et al., 2013, Vlachos & Bogdanovic, 2013) could be eliminated by applying the VSM in conjunction with support tools.

Lima & Zawislak (2003) point out that waste should be identified in the critical stages of transportation where parts are transported most frequently.

Teichgraber & Bucourt (2012) report cases in which loss due to waiting can occur due to a lack of medication, occupancy in operating rooms, errors and delays in scheduling.

Carter et al. (2012) highlights the long length of stay in hospital and patient waiting times as the main losses, while Teichgraber & Bucourt (2012) highlight losses related to excessive patient movement in the corridors, floors and care units of a hospital.

In the case of industries, the majority of organizations that have cases of transport waste (Salgado et al., 2009; Jiménez et al., 2012; Marques et al., 2013; Bauer et al., 2014; Prashar, 2014), implement improvements using forklifts and conveyor belts, which, in reality, only improve the transport activity, with 'real improvements' being considered only those that reduce the need for the transport function of the system (Shingo, 1996a, 1996b). Also in this sector, high defect rates (Roldan & Miyake,

2004; Singh et al., 2006; Salgado et al., 2009; Vinodh et al., 2010; Matt et al., 2013; Vinodh et al., 2013; Haefner et al., 2014; Prashar, 2014), processing losses (Roldan & Miyake, 2004; Bevilacqua et al., 2008; Salgado et al., 2009; Al-Tahat, 2010; Singh et al., 2010; Garg & Naidoo, 2012; Singh & Singh, 2013), high installation costs, logistics costs, waste in the assembly phase (Lima & Zawislak, 2003) and rework (Haefner et al., 2014) are motivators for using VSM.

For the hotel sector, Vlachos & Bogdanovic (2013) indicate motivational factors for both the booking process and the process of purchasing accommodation. The overbooking of vacancies, the inadequate processing of administrative activities, the unnecessary movement of guests and employees and high defect rates are examples cited by the author, while in *health care,* Teichgraber & Bucourt (2012) list the inaccurate ordering, delivery or implementation of prostheses, the excess of personnel or material used in the process, as examples of processing loss and highlight inspection, in this case, as a loss by defect that should be considered as a non-value-added process.

When it comes to time-related factors, the VSM is recognized as a method with the potential to bring about improvements in *lead time*, since the existence of a high *lead time* tends to mean relevance and high costs (Ferro, 2005). *Lead time* is a component of planning and is essential information in the customer service process (Kosaka, 2015).

Production strategies focused on reducing *lead times* allow for greater efficiency in the production process, greater flexibility and faster deliveries (Oliveira & Philippi, 2013).

Chen et al. (2013) reports on the need to reduce *lead times* in a distribution center, while Lian & Van Landeghem (2007) and Jiménez et al. (2012) state that excessive *lead times* compromise delivery dates and generate customer dissatisfaction.

Yu et al. (2013) reveals that a disorganized process and unbalanced production line leads to significant waste such as high lead times, high cycle times and high *takt-times*. When value-added times are higher than *takt-time*, it is not possible to produce the quantity of units needed to meet the pace of sales (Lima & Zawislak, 2003).

Singh et al. (2011) mentions that one of the main difficulties encountered in a railroad industry is to reduce high cycle *times and lead times*, and that the VSM, unlike conventional techniques, can help identify waste in the process and separate activities with and without added value.

Table 5 - Description of the motivation categories according to the authors.

Factors	**Author's description**
Weather-related factors:	
High *lead times*	Hines & Rich (1997); Hines et al. (1999); Lima & Zawislak (2003); Kaale et al. (2005); Abdulmalek & Rajgopal (2007); Lawrence et al. (2007); Lian & Van Landeghem (2007); Barber & Tietje (2008); Bevilacqua et al. (2008); Lasa et al. (2008); Serrano et al. (2008); Seth et al. (2008); Salgado et al. (2009); Wang et al. (2009); Yu et al. (2009); L'Hommedieu & Kappeler (2010); Vinodh et al. (2010); Garrett & Lee (2011); Kuhlang et al. (2011); Nepal et al. (2011); Singh et al. (2011); Duranik et al. (2012); Jiménez et al. (2012); Rahani & Al-Ashraf (2012); Wong et al. (2012); Chen et al. (2013); Tanco et al. (2013); Vinodh et al. (2013); Abdelhadi & Shakoor (2014); Brown et al. (2014); Cevikcan & Durmusoglu (2014); Faulkner & Badurdeen (2014); Heinzen et al. (2014); Khurum et al. (2014); Librelato et al. (2014); Müller et al. (2014); Tyagi et al. (2014).
High cycle times	Lummus et al. (2006); Singh et al. (2006); Adrian et al. (2007); Singh & Sharma (2009); Al-Tahat (2010); Chen et al. (2010); Vinodh et al. (2010); Gurumurthy & Kodali (2011); Lu et al. (2011); Singh et al. (2011); Hofacker et al. (2012); Singh & Singh (2013); Souza et al. (2013); Vinodh et al. (2013); Yu et al. (2013); Abdelhadi & Shakoor (2014); Faulkner & Badurdeen (2014); Jasti & Sharma (2014); Librelato et al. (2014).
No *takt-time* service	Lima & Zawslak (2003); Matt (2008); Serrano et al. (2008); Abdelhadi & Shakoor (2014).
Non-added value time	Lima & Zawslak (2003); Serrano et al. (2008); Jiménez et al. (2012); Heinzen et al. (2014).
High R&D *lead time*	Wang et al. (2011).
Factors related to the Supply Chain:	
Difficulty in relationship with suppliers	Hines et al. (1998); Teichgraber & de Bucourt (2012); Susilawati et al. (2015).
Losses in supply chain links	Hines et al. (1998); Folinas et al. (2013).
Factors related to production systems:	
Lack of flexibility (Product/process)	Hines et al. (1998); Holweg (2005); Gibbons et al. (2012).
Long *setup* times	Braglia et al. (2006).
Equipment downtime	Agyapong-Koduaa et al. (2012); Garg & Naido (2012); Basu & Dan (2014)
Waiting	Roldan & Miyake (2004); Lummus et al. (2006); Salgado et al. (2009);

	Singh & Sharma (2009); Wee & Wu (2009); Grove at al. (2010); Ng et al. al. (2010); Singh et al. (2010); Cima et al. (2011); Cookson et al. (2011); Gurumurthy & Kodali (2011); Schwarz et al. (2011); Carter et al. (2012); Chen et al. (2012); Hydes et al. (2012); Xie & Peng (2012); Chen et al. (2013); Chiarini (2013); Tanco et al. (2013); Vlachos & Bogdanovic (2013); Jasti & Sharma (2014); Khurum et al. (2014); Matt (2014).
Processing	Roldan & Miyake (2004); Bevilacqua et al. (2008); Salgado et al. (2009); Yu et al. (2009); Al-Tahat (2010); Grove et al. (2010); L'Hommedieu & Kappeler (2010); Ng et al. (2010); Singh et al. (2010); Garg & Naido (2012); Hydes et al. (2012); Teichgraber & Bucourt (2012); Wong et al. (2012); Singh & Singh (2013), Vlachos & Bogdanovic (2013).
Transportation	Salgado et al. (2009); L'Hommedieu & Kappeler (2010); Cima et al. (2011); Carter et al. (2012); Chen et al. (2012); Jiménez et al. (2012); Chen at al. (2013); Chiarini (2013); Marques et al. (2013); Vlachos & Bogdanovic (2013); Bauer et al. (2014); Prashar (2014).
Defects/Quality	Roldan & Miyake (2004); Singh et al. (2006); Matt (2008); Salgado et al. (2009); Vinodh et al. (2010); Garrett & Lee (2011); Teichgraber & Bucourt (2012); Matt et al. (2013); Vinodh et al. (2013); Vlachos & Bogdanovic (2013); Yu et al. (2013); Haefner et al. (2014); Prashar (2014).
Movement	Alvarez et al. (2009); Hydes et al. (2012); Tabanli & Ertay (2013).
Overproduction	Vlachos & Bogdanovic (2013).
Others:	
Health and safety risk	Chiarini (2012); Chiarini (2014).

4.2.4. Implementation

The steps adopted in the research that serve as the basis for implementing the VSM are: *(i)* setting objectives; *(ii)* identifying losses; *(iii)* planning and executing the *kaizens* and; *(iv)* analyzing the *kaizens,* generating the current value stream map and the future value stream map as products.

In order to apply the VSM, it is necessary to establish objectives and targets aligned with the business strategy and the managers of the unit under study, as highlighted in the case of Hines et al. (1999), who selects a group made up of managers, whose key role is to guarantee critical targets that must be pursued in the program.

The goal of increasing inventory turnover, reducing *lead time* to five weeks, improving sales forecast accuracy by 45% and improving delivery performance by 95% are defined for this case study (Hines et al., 1999). Teichgraber & Bucourt (2012) identifies all non-value-added activities in the hospital materials procurement process, while Carter et al. (2012) aims to reduce patient waiting times by 50%.

For Chen et al. (2013), the aim is to analyze losses in the receiving, storage, sorting, packaging and delivery operations using Lean concepts, as well as using RFID technology. Once the objectives have been established, data must be collected to identify waste. In the case of

Hines & Rich (1997), preliminary interviews with managers were carried out in order to identify existing waste in the value chain. In addition, the author highlights the importance of gaining managers' points of view by understanding the industrial structure, regardless of which wastes need to be removed.

This selection of tools is achieved by giving the interviewees a description of the overview of each of the wastes as well as an explanation of what is meant by the structure of the factory. At this stage, it is necessary to reformulate the description of the seven wastes in terms that are more appropriate for the industry under study (Hines & Rich, 1997).

In the case of Lima & Zawislak (2003), seven companies in the automotive chain were interviewed in a multiple case study. Employees from production, quality, sales and purchasing were interviewed. The cycle times of the production stages observed were measured and *setup* times were obtained from company information. After visiting the areas involved and collecting information on the four topics studied (general data, sales relations, production and supplies) from the respective managers, a map was drawn of the current state of each company with regard to the product under study (Lima & Zawislak, 2003).

Singh et al. (2011) highlights data collection being carried out through discussions with workers, supervisors and managers, as well as considering data such as historical sales for analysis, while Tabanli & Ertay (2013) present a questionnaire with six questions related to the production system with information regarding takt-time, critical points in the value chain, product *mix* and processes that require improvement.

Carter et al. (2012) mentions that direct observation, meetings with hospital staff and *feedback* helped to sustain the support of managers during the initial development phase of the project. In the case of Vlachos & Bogdanovic (2013), the main research method is quantitative analysis of empirical data collected through questionnaires sent to hotel managers.

Specifically, small and medium-sized hotels in 19 European Union (EU) countries were examined. The variables included in the study were the number of lean practices employed, the sectors in which they were applied and the perceptions of management in terms of accounting, customer loyalty and employee performance. A Likert scale was chosen to measure the attitudes of the questionnaire respondents (Clason & Dormody, 1993). The current state map is carried out after data collection and consists of a linear process of classifying value-added activity, non-value-added activity and non-value-added activity, but is necessary in order to obtain the total *lead time of* a process. The current state map creates a common understanding of how activities actually work in the value stream, so that people can work together to identify and solve problems by proposing improvements.

A value stream map provides a model for implementing lean manufacturing concepts, illustrating how the flow of information and materials should operate (Sullivan et al., 2002). Firstly, non-value-added activities must be removed from the system while waste related to non-value-added but necessary activities requires radical changes to the process (Tabanli & Ertay, 2013). In the current state map, the product family, process data and physical flows must be determined (Lasa et al., 2008).

Hines & Rich (1997) analyze the flow of value upstream to the point where the goods are available for distribution and, like Sullivan et al. (2002), define the family of products to be studied according to the calculation of sales volume using the Pareto chart. On the other hand, Lima & Zawislak (2003) select parts with higher defect rates during production or customer returns and products that represent higher turnover for the company as the object of study, while Braglia et al. (2006) select a product line that represents 60% of overall production. Information flow includes how the sales forecast reaches the unit and how the sales forecast is delivered to the supplier. Physical flows are related to the changes made to the raw material to produce the finished product. Information on delivery times, quantity of raw materials, operating time, equipment failure time, storage points, cycle time and number of operators per shift are examples of information that must be collected from the current state (Tabanli & Ertay, 2013).

The customer, supplier, processes, information flow, process metrics and timeline are considered as zones of the value stream in the current state map. Another important factor to note is that before mapping the current state, a value stream must be selected and the mapping level decided.

In the case of Yu et al. (2013), the two decisions were interrelated. When the door-to-door production flow was looked at in relation to a value stream, mapping could only be done at the station level, since a single map covering all the tasks carried out within each station would be unwieldy.

The value stream map, at a high level, provides a big picture of the process, but does not show small details of the operations. The map cannot be used for root cause analysis and future map formulation. In contrast, a station can be seen as a value stream with the previous station as the supplier station and the next station as the customer station. The problem with mapping at this level is that the value stream may not be stable. For this study, Yu et al. (2013) reports that two-level maps were used simultaneously to identify waste and develop solutions.

For the case of Huang & Liu (2005), a logical algorithm symbology was used as a complementary tool. The process is presented using the current state map, with the upper part of the block corresponding to the process name and the lower part corresponding to the data box. In the data box, data related to, for example, cycle time is used to record the processing time in the process while triangles correspond to the stock and storage area. The reason why the logical symbols are added to the VSM methodology is that the traditional VSM does not show the temporal precedence between different processes. Through the current state map, losses are also identified.

Carter et al. (2012) states that instead of analyzing system data to identify waste, icons are used on the value stream map to indicate waste within the process. The losses considered in the VSM are overproduction, stock loss, transportation loss, waiting loss, handling loss, processing loss and defect loss. In the loss identification stage, Jiménez et al. (2012) reports losses such as high stock levels, high production *lead times* and a high flow of unnecessary information in the production system and that, in order to reduce and eliminate these wastes, a series of questions should be asked to facilitate understanding of the current flow and establishment of a future process flow.

Chen et al. (2013) emphasizes the high waiting and transport times in the distribution process of a DC, where the value-added time is only about 0.7% of the total operation time. Two major wastes are thus identified and can be reduced or eliminated following the discussion. In summary, the current operations of both warehousing and distribution are inefficient, as a result of poor management and slow manual operations, which lead to low throughput, long waiting times and high labor costs.

Carter et al. (2012) highlights the identification of waste in an emergency department related to defects such as incorrect surgical procedure and medication error, waste related to overproduction such as antibiotics administered due to viral infection and waste related to waiting, where the patient waits for beds to be available in the emergency department for admission. The author also highlights waste related to unnecessary movement, such as long distances between stages of the administrative process, waste related to stock, such as the supply of excessive stock to guarantee the availability of the hospital product, and waste related to transportation, such as the frequent moving of patients in the emergency room. In the planning and elaboration stage of *kaizens*, an action plan is drawn up, as in the case of Sullivan et al. (2002), which determines what changes are necessary to achieve the future state. The concept of continuous improvement is based on *Kaizen* and presupposes the ability to identify the causes of problems and implement solutions (Slack, 1999). The search for continuous improvement in production takes place with the aim of analyzing the form and performance measures of the process (Slack, 1999).

The tools used in conjunction with the VSM should be selected according to their immediate usefulness to the company (Tanco et al., 2013). The VSM provides an overview of the value chain and helps to identify opportunities for improvement. However, in some cases (Hines et al., 1998; Hines et al., 1999; Huang & Liu, 2005; Abdulmalek & Rajgopal, 2007; Adrian et al., 2007; Lawrence et al., 2007; Lian & Van Landeghem, 2007; Bevilacqua et al., 2008; Alvarez et al., 2009; Wang et al., 2009; Yu et al.., 2009; Al-Tahat, 2010; Chen et al., 2010; Cima et al., 2011; Gurumurthy & Kodali, 2011, Yang & Lu, 2011, Lu et al., 2011; Nepal et al., 2011, Schwarz et al., 2011; Agyapong-Koduaa et al., 2012; Carter et al., 2012; Chen et al., 2012; Chiarini, 2012; Duranik et al..., 2012; Jiménez et al., 2012; Rahani & Al-Ashraf, 2012; Xie & Peng, 2012; Chen et al., 2013; Chiarini, 2013; Matt et al., 2013; Souza et al., 2013; Tabanli & Ertay, 2013; Tanco et al., 2013; Vinodh et al., 2013; Yu et al., 2013; Chiarini, 2014; Haefner et al..., 2014; Jasti & Sharma, 2014; Khurum et al., 2014; Librelato et al., 2014; Prashar, 2014; Tyagi et al., 2014), and especially at this stage of the process, researchers suggest other tools to be used in conjunction with the VSM. Table 6 describes the authors according to the use of the support tool.

Table 6 - Description of authors according to support tool

Support tool	**Authors' description**
Simulation	Huang & Liu (2005); Lian & Van Landeghem (2007); Bevilacqua et al. (2008); Wang et al. (2009); Yu et al. (2009); Gurumurthy & Kodali (2011); Yang & Lu (2011); Lu et al. (2011); Agyapong-Koduaa et al. (2012); Xie & Peng (2012); Tanco et. al (2013); Vinodh et. al (2013); Khurum et al. (2014).
Kanban	Hines et al. (1998); Alvarez et al. (2009); Chen et al. (2012); Duranik et al. (2012); Jiménez et al. (2012); Che et al. (2013); Tabanli & Ertay (2013); Librelato et al. (2014).
Kaizen	Chen et al. (2010); Jiménez et al. (2012); Rahani & Al-Ashraf (2012); Jasti & Sharma (2014); Prashar (2014).
Six Sigma	Cima et al. (2011); Chiarini (2012); Souza et al. (2013); Haefner et al. (2014).
PMS	Hines et al. (1998); Abdulmalek & Rajgopal (2007); Jiménez et al. (2012); Chiarini (2014).
Ishikawa diagram	Carter et al. (2012); Chiarini (2012); Haefner et al. (2014) ; Librelato et al. (2014).
SMED	Hines et al. (1998); Jiménez et al. (2012); Chiarini (2014).
5 Whys	Chen et al. (2010); Carter et al. (2012); Prashar (2014).
5S	Hines et al. (1998); Yu et al. (2013); Chiarini (2014).

Pareto chart	Hines et al. (1999); Sullivan et al. (2002); Lima & Zawislak (2003)
Spaghetti diagram	Chiarini (2013); Tanco et al. (2013).
Cycle time planning	Hines et al. (1998); Yu et al. (2013).
RFID	Chen et al. (2013); Tabanli & Ertay (2013).
Theory of constraints	Lawrence et al. (2007); Librelato et al. (2014).
Statistical test	Nepal et al. (2011); Schwarz et al. (2011).
SIPOC	Carter et al. (2012)
Automation	Al-Tahat (2010)
Balanced scorecard	Adrian et al. (2007)
Brainstorming	Chiarini (2012)
DMAIC	Chiarini (2012)
Elimination of losses	Hines et al. (1998)
FMEA	Chiarini (2012)
Variation management	Yu et al. (2013)
Jidoka	Hines et al. (1998)
Relationship matrix	Matt et al. (2013)
OEE	Tanco et al. (2013)
Activity sheet	Chiarini (2013)
Poka-yoke	Hines et al. (1998)
Problem solving	Hines et al. (1998)
Management board in sight	Hines et al. (1998)
Simplex	Huang & Liu (2005)
5W2H	Chiarini (2012)

Source: Prepared by the author.

Carter et al. (2012) reports that the SIPOC tool (*suppliers, inputs, process, outputs, customers) and* problem-solving tools (five whys and *Ishikawa* diagram) were easily transported to the project.

The SIPOC tool was used to define the scope of the project by defining the individual characteristics of the high-level process. The SIPOC tool was essential in the hospital sector due to the lack of standard terminology among healthcare professionals. In addition, the large volume of complex processes that needed to be dealt with in the hospital and the anxiety of the team members to fix all the problems in the system at once were additional factors that could generate problems within the project and which, in turn, were solved by the tool.

Using the SIPOC tool, a standard definition was created for the process steps. The author also reports that the problem-solving tools (five whys and Ishikawa diagram) are easily transferable and are effective methods for stimulating team discussion.

Haefner et al. (2014) cites that the main causes of each defect are identified through Ishikawa analysis and the result is illustrated in the corresponding text boxes under each production process. An important analysis in the study is that both the pure VSM and combined VSM approaches show well-distributed results (Figure 10), which reinforces the need to re-evaluate the VSM and indicates, overall, the need for a complementary tool to the VSM that can quantify gains during the planning and early evaluation phases (Gurumurthy & Kodali, 2011).

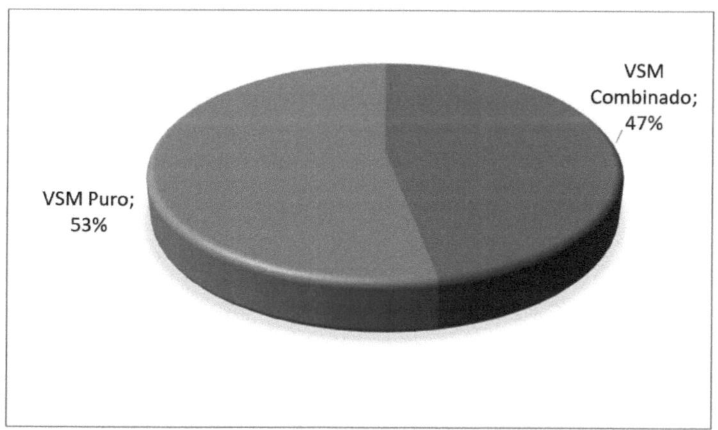

Figure 10 - Percentage of VSM approach in publications.
Source: Prepared by the author.

As an example, Tanco et al. (2013) uses discrete event simulation *software* to simulate the current state map and the future state map. This allows simulation to deal with uncertainties and create dynamic views of intermediate stock levels, machine efficiency and different time measures (Abdulmalek & Rajgopal, 2007; Serrano et al., 2008). Reinforcing VSM with simulation is important to provide information that cannot be provided by using VSM alone due to its static nature (Mc Donald et al., 2002; Lian & Van Landeghem, 2007).

Through support tools and *kaizens*, quick solutions and continuous efforts are made to improve the practice of the system (Slack, 1999).

Haefner et al. (2014) points out that relevant quality performance indicators have been determined for process improvements.

In the case of Tanco et al. (2013), daily shipments of finished products, preparation of sales forecasts, definition of the packaging and products required, a U-shaped layout and evaluation of the quality of packaging are examples of improvements that should be implemented in the system. The author points out that shipping finished products every day would reduce stock from 5 days to 0.5 days. Drawing up a sales forecast based on the previous year's consumption would make customer service more accurate and reduce stock levels. The time study showed that it was possible to improve productivity by optimizing work and improving the *layout*. The improvement would reduce the unnecessary movement of the operator, who in turn would work at the pace imposed by the line.

Improvements related to increasing machine efficiency are also suggested in the study (Tanco et al. 2013).

Chen et al. (2012) cites the development of a receiving schedule, the implementation of an EDI (*Electronic Data Interchange*) system based on the Internet, the integration of the RFDI with the operation's system and a reduction in the time taken to approve the inspection procedure as ways of improving the system. The author points out that by drawing up a receiving schedule according to the manufacturer's delivery time, the operator can organize the inspection schedule in advance, carry out the inspection on time, the document can be approved and sent back to the distribution center the next day.

Once the processes of the above operation are changed, the time for accepting and storing goods can be reduced by 95%. In relation to the implementation of the Internet-based EDI system, operators and the entire information flow can communicate directly with each other in real time, while the integration of RFID technology with the information system will allow the identities and data of RFID tags attached to products and pallets to be captured automatically (Chen et al., 2012). After defining the *kaizens* to be executed, the future state map is drawn up, which will provide the guidelines for establishing value, work, flow and management. Also at this stage, the process metrics are compared on the current state map and the future state map.

Sullivan et al. (2002) emphasizes that the future state map uses the same process steps as the current state map. However, with the identification of waste, the future state map has an advantage in production time of 16 hours. By reducing in-process stock, inventory costs and defect costs can be reduced. These savings can then be used to determine whether it is economically advantageous to implement the lean manufacturing concepts embedded in the future state (Sullivan et al., 2002).

In order to outline the new process, Roldan & Miyake (2004) describe that, with the critical visions and proposals gathered from each element, they sought to direct the resources to what is really important for the end customer of the process, using the future state map. The new flow outlined already provides for the elimination of activities considered to have no added value in order to make better use of existing resources.

Salgado et al. (2009) presents a map of the future state with the implementation of improvement proposals. The future state map represents the ideal situation of the product development plan of the company studied. As a result, the waste balloons are eliminated, since the future state time of the process is the current state time without the waste. Thus, the future state map shows how much the company can improve by eliminating waste.

Teichgraber & de Bucourt (2012) describe that the creation of the future state map presents a progressive elimination of waste by means of a consignment stock, which is completely operated by the supplier. The future state applies a different stock control system to the previous one.

Lima & Zawislak (2003) point out that the future state map sought to optimize the *lead time* and the value-added time of the line, in order to meet the *takt-time of* the product studied. The author emphasizes that the choice of these production performance gauges is due to their close relationship with the company's supply capacity. The VSM has proven to be a practical and original tool, with many attributes that can improve production systems (Tanco et al., 2013).

However, it should be made clear that its application in practice can be difficult, as in the case of Yu et al. (2013) who, although the future state map shows the ideal state of the production line, it is not possible to execute the entire lean system at the same time. In fact, different attitudes of the operation towards change are highlighted in this study, which justifies the variation in the progression of improvements. Management had to consistently adjust the VSM implementation plan based on the actual situation in order to maintain improvements on the production lines. Limitations such as these have encouraged some researchers to question the use of the tool and to use other ways of improving it (Lian & Van Landeghem, 2007; Gurumurthy & Kodali, 2011).

It is clear that the VSM has some restrictions in its application. As a broader limitation of the method, there is a lack of connection with corporate strategy and the market, and a lack of connection with human resources issues such as organizational culture and communication. There is a lack of understanding of how the method generates results and how the method can be implemented, as its application is generally very time-consuming (Hines et al., 1998).

With regard to problems concerning the general environment of use, the VSM has a gap in understanding between what the tool is looking for and how it can be achieved. The method loses subjective and qualitative information with formal analysis (Hines et al., 1998). Problems associated with the method where wasted energy, human potential, information management and finite capacity planning are not considered should also be highlighted (Hines et al., 1998).

4.2.5. Outputs and results

The outputs, based on the articles selected for study, from production processes and services were classified as loss reduction, human resources/work/increased productivity, delivery *lead time,* customer service index, cycle time, risk reduction, flexibility (*mix* and products), sustainability/environment and reduction in the flow of information in the process.

Table 7 shows the segmentation of the research by group of authors. The main results refer to the reduction of the seven wastes, in particular the reduction of waiting time, the reduction of processing time and the reduction of stock levels.

This result is consistent with the literature, as Hines & Rich (1997) show a low correlation and usefulness of the activity mapping process in reducing overproduction and defects. Huang & Liu (2005) present the elimination of stock losses and *setup* losses as the outputs of the process, while Braglia et al. (2006) emphasize that the reduction in the number of *setups* is as high as 50%.

Lian & Van Landeghem (2007) show that the main result of applying VSM to the production process is a 48% reduction in *lead time.* In *health care*, Carter et al. (2012) show that in order to obtain consistent results with VSM, eight lessons learned must be followed: *(i)* the *Lean* process assists in building a partnership between employees from various sectors; *(ii)* obtaining and maintaining institutional support is necessary and challenging; *(iii)* obtaining *feedback* from all team members is fundamental for *Lean* Manufacturing to be successful; *(iv)* choosing a manageable pilot project is key to influencing the use of lean production throughout the project; *(v) lean* production tools can be adapted to other hospitals and are effective in a low-resource health system; *(vi)* several Lean Production tools focused on problem-solving worked well in a low-resource system without modification; *(vii) Lean* Production highlighted that major changes don't need a lot of resources and; *(viii)* despite different levels of resources, causes of system deficiencies are similar in all health systems, but need unique solutions suited to each clinical situation. These lessons lead to customer satisfaction results and increased profits.

Sullivan et al. (2002) states that with the implementation of the VSM, tangible benefits include inventory savings, space reduction and higher product quality. Intangible benefits include greater flexibility and increased learning. There is also an advantage in the ability to meet demand within shorter delivery times. The results classified in the survey were: profit, customer satisfaction, *market share* and the environment. A direct impact on results, measured by profit margin and market share, was absent from the articles reviewed in the research. It is possible that there are indirect effects on the results, as the VSM is an operational tool that can only be applied to a specific process or service.

However, Chiarini (2014) as well as Faulkner & Bardurdeen (2014), report positive effects of VSM on the environment while Hydes et al. (2012) and Souza et al. (2013) report better customer service as results.

Tanco et al. (2013) observed a drastic reduction in customer service *lead times*, leading to increased customer satisfaction. In addition, the reduction in waiting time could easily translate into lower financial costs and lower inventory cost management and, consequently, an increase in profit.

Even though the application of the VSM by the authors researched is proven with quantitative and qualitative results, the research obtained little objective correlation of the outputs generated by the tool, and there is a need for articles with a greater dimension of the scope of the research. In this context, the extension of traditional research into the VSM must reach and measure the results generated. Output indicators should be converted into broader organizational indicators according to the strategic level of companies.

Table 7 - Description of research results by author

Type of results	**Authors' description**
Loss reduction:	
1. Defects 2. *Overproduction/takt-time*	Singh et al. (2006); Matt (2008); Vinodh et al. (2010); Tabanli & Ertay (2013); Vinodh et al. (2013); Prashar (2014).
3. Transportation	Gurumurthy & Kodali (2011); Abdelhadi & Shakoor (2014); Jasti & Sharma (2014).
4. Waiting 5. Stock 6. Movement 7. Processing	Chen et al. (2012); Bauer et al. (2014); Jasti & Sharma (2014) Roldan & Miyake (2004); Huang & Liu (2005); Kaale et al. (2005); Lummus et al. (2006); Singh & Sharma (2009); Ng et al. (2010); Singh et al. (2010); Cima et al. (2011); Cookson et al. (2011); Schwartz et al. (2011); Chen et al. (2012); Hydes et al. (2012); Rahani & al-Ashraf (2012); Xie & Peng (2012); Chiarini (2013); Khurum et al. (2014).
Other results:	

Human resources/work/increased productivity	Huang & Liu (2005); Bevilacqua et al. (2008); Alvarez et al. (2009); Singh & Sharma (2009); Singh et al. (2010); Vinodh et al. (2010); Nepal et al. (2011); Singh et al. (2011); Yang & Lu (2011); Chiarini (2012); Duranik et al. (2012); Jiménez et al. (2012); Teichgraber & de Bucourt (2012); Chen et al. (2013); Souza et al. (2013); Singh & Singh (2013); Tabanli & Ertay (2013); Tanco et al. (2013); Vinodh et al. (2013); Prashar (2014); Librelato et al. (2014).
Delivery *lead time*	Alvarez et al. (2009); Wee & Wu (2009)
customer service index	Lima & Zawislak (2003); Braglia (2006); Abdumalek & Rajgopal (2007); Lian & Van Landeghem (2007); Lasa et al. (2008); Salgado et al. (2009); Singh & Shama (2009); Wee & Wu (2009); Al-Tahat (2010); Singh et al. (2010); Vinodh et al. (2010); Garrett & Lee (2011); Gurumurthy & Kodali (2011); Nepal et al. (2011); Duranik et al. (2012); Hofacker et al. (2012); Jiménez et al. (2012); Chen et al. (2013); Singh & Singh (2013); Tanco et al. (2013); Yu et al. (2013); Cevikcan & Durmusoglu (2014); Faulkner & Bardurdeen (2014); Jasti & Sharma (2014); Khurum et al. (2014); Müller et al. (2014).
Cycle time	Lawrence et al. (2007); Matt (2008); Salgado et al. (2009); Singh & Shama (2009); Wee & Wu (2009); Ng et al. (2010); Singh et al. (2010); Cima et al. (2011); Schwartz et al. (2011); Singh et al. (2011); Agyapong-Koduaa et al. (2012); Duranik et al. (2012); Hydes et al. (2012); Wong et al. (2012); Jiménez et al. (2012); Tabanli & Ertay (2013); Yu et al. (2013); Basu & Dan (2014); Bauer et al. (2014); Jasti & Sharma (2014); Khurum et al. (2014); Prashar (2014).
Risk reduction	Hines et al. (1999); Vinodh et al. (2010); Chen et al. (2012); Vinodh et al. (2013); Faulkner & Bardurdeen (2014) Hydes et al. (2012); Souza et al. (2013).
Flexibility (*mix* and products)	Yu et al. (2009); Al-Tahat (2010); Chen et al. (2010); Vinodh et al. (2010); Lu et al. (2011); Singh et al. (2011); Hofacker et al. (2012); Singh & Singh (2013); Vinodh et al. (2013); Yu et al. (2013); Abdelhadi & Shakoor (2014); Basu & Dan (2014). Chiarini (2012).
Sustainability/environment	Holweg (2005); Matt (2008).
Reduction in information flow	Chiarini (2014); Faulkner & Bardurdeen (2014).
	Jiménez et al. (2012).

Source: Prepared by the author.

5. Conclusions and final considerations

The field of application of the VSM has been evolving and growing since the 1990s and has spread to various sectors of the economy (manufacturing, services, logistics and *healthcare*).

Its application has been reported in terms of pure VSM and VSM combined with other lean manufacturing or management tools as a whole. In the 91 articles researched, there was a near absence of a literature review, justifying the need for systematic research on the subject.

The justifications that guarantee that the VSM is really effective are evidenced by the measurable outputs, mostly around losses. Its main characteristic is that it is suitable for a broader analysis of the chain, taking into account the activities of an entire process and the customer's requirements, even though it sometimes lacks the help of other lean production management tools.

When it comes to the aspects that VSM theory must improve in order to become a benchmark tool, not all efforts to implement the tool are simple to execute, as some examples of case studies report increased costs during the project due to the need for changes to be implemented in a case of re-engineering for EPC (*Engineering. Procurement and Construction)* projects, with an estimated payback of 4 years, *Procurement and Construction*) projects, with an estimated payback of 4 years, and a negative NPV (Net Present Value) obtained in a VSM project for an integrated patient care control system.

In some cases, the implementation of the Lean Production flow can be very demanding for companies that have few resources, while in other cases, caution is advised when implementing the VSM, as its implementation could be time-consuming and expensive. With this in mind, the authors cite limitations essentially in three areas: *(i)* the difficulty of applying the VSM in the public sector; *(ii)* the difficulty of generalizing the tool as evidenced in case studies and; *(iii) the* few detailed cases of investigation. The *framework* developed is essential for synthesizing the literature review of the articles selected for the study.

The elimination of waste in a process or production chain is evident, followed by the reduction of *lead times*, as the most frequent motivation. The most frequently pursued wastes are waste in stock, waiting, processing and transportation, with a few motivations related to handling, overproduction and health and safety risks.

It is important to note in the research that the implementation process considered simulation, *kanban* and *kaizen* as the main support tools, even though it cited around 32 lean production management tools in all.

Still in the process of implementation, the broader limitations of the method were observed, due to gaps between corporate strategy and the market and gaps related to the method's connection with human resources issues such as organizational culture and communication. There are limitations in terms of how the method generates results, how it can be implemented and how long it takes to apply.

The VSM neglects waste associated with wasted energy, human potential, information management and capacity planning. Other limitations of the VSM found in the systematic review can be classified as: *(i)* the need for the tool to be related to the market and aligned with corporate strategic planning, since the focus of the VSM is only the mapping of losses in a process, and even if it includes the relationship with the supplier and the customer in the value chain, it does not consider the organizational objectives and goals and strategic planning. The impact on the strategic indicators proposed by the *balanced scorecard* was not found in the literature researched; *(ii)* the absence of a *framework* for implementation agreed upon by the authors, which in turn drew attention in the research, since although the steps for its implementation were clear, the method was not described in the articles; in addition to *(iii)* the absence of details of the current state map and future state map in the works researched, where only the maps were presented and not their rich elaboration process.

As a recommendation for future research, this study could be extended to: *(i) the development* of a case study, action research and a *survey* of the Lean Production tools to be applied in conjunction with the VSM for each of the sectors observed, contextualizing them and; *(ii)* the development of the VSM *framework* for the *helthcare sector* due to its growing application in the sector, which justifies the dedication to an in-depth research review of the literature for the sector.

6. Bibliographical references

ABDELHADI, A.; SHAKOOR, M. **Studying the efficiency of inpatient and outpatient pharmacies using lean manufacturing.** Leadership in Health Services, Vol. 27 n°.3, pp. 255-267, 2014.

ABDULMALEK, F. A.; RAJGOPAL, J. **Analyzing the benefits of lean manufacturing and value stream mapping via simulation: a process sector case study.** International Journal of Production Economics, Vol. 107, pp. 223-236, 2007.

ADRIAN, E.; CORONADO, M.; ANDREW, C. L. **Evaluating operations flexibility in industrial supply chains to support build- to- order initiatives.** Business Process Management Journal, Vol.13 n°.4, pp. 572-587, 2007.

AGYAPONG-KODUAA; K.; AJAEFOBI, J. O.; WESTON, R. H.; RATCHEV, S. **Development of a multi-product cost and value stream modelling methodology.** International Journal of Production Research, Vol. 50 n°.22, pp. 6431-6456, 2012.

AL-TAHAT, M. D. **Effective design and analysis of pattern making process-using value stream mapping.** Journal of Applied Sciences, Vol. 10 n°.11, pp. 878 - 886, 2010.

ALVAREZ, R.; CALVO, R.; PENA, M. M.; DOMINGO, R. **Redesigning an assembly line through lean manufacturing tools.** The International Journal of Advanced Manufacturing Technology, Vol. 43 n°.9/10, pp. 949-958, 2009.

ANTUNES, J. **Sistemas de Produçâo: Conceitos e Práticas para Projeto e Gestao da Produçâo Enxuta.** Porto Alegre: Bookman, 2008.

BARBER, C. S.; TIETJE, B. C. **Research agenda of value stream mapping the sales process.** Journal of Personal Selling & Sales Management, Vol. 28 n°.2, pp. 155-165, 2008.

BASU, P.; DAN. P. K. **Capacity augmentation with VSM methodology for lean manufacturing.** International Journal of Lean Six Sigma, Vol. 5 n°.3, pp. 279-292, 2014.

BAUER, W.; GANSCHAR, O.; GERLACH, S. **Development of a method for visualization and evaluation of production logistics in a multi-variant production.** Procedia CIRP, Vol. 17, pp. 481-486, 2014.

BERTO, R. M. V. S.; NAKANO, D. N. A. **Produçâo cientifica nos anais do encontro nacional de engenharia de produçâo: Um Ievantamento de métodos e tipos de pesquisa.** Produçâo, Vol. 9 n°.2, pp. 65-76, 2000.

BERTRAND, J. W. M.; FRANSOO, J. C. **Modeling and simulation: operations management research methodology using quantitative modeling.** International Journal of Operations and Production Management, Vol. 22 n°.2, pp. 241-264, 2002.

BEVILACQUA, M.; CIARAPICA, F. E.; GIACCHETTA, G. **Value stream mapping in project management: A case study.** Project Management Journal, Vol. 39 n°.3, pp. 110-124, 2008.

BHAMU, J.; SANGWAN, K. S. **Lean manufacturing: literature review and research issues.** International Journal of Operations & Production Management, Vol. 34 n°.7, pp. 876-940, 2014.

BORNIA, A. C. **Managerial cost analysis: application in modern companies.**

Porto Alegre: Bookman, 2002.

BOWERSOX, D. J.; CLOSS, D. **Simulated product sales forecasting.** s.l.:East Lansing: MSU Business Studies, 1979.

BRAGLIA, M.; CARMIGNANI, G.; ZAMMORI, F. **A new value stream mapping approach for complex production systems.** International Journal of Production Research, Vol. 44 n°.18/19, pp. 3929-3952, 2006.

BROWN, A.; AMUNDSON, J.; BADURDEEN, F. **Sustainable value stream mapping (Sus-VSM) in different manufacturing system configurations: application case studies.** Journal of Cleaner Production, Vol. 85, pp. 164-179, 2014.

CARTER; P. M.; DESMOND, J. S.; AKANBOBNAAB, C.; OTENG, R. A.; ROMINSKI, S. D.; BARSAN, W. G.; CUNNINGHAM, R. M. **Optimizing clinical**

operations as part of a global emergency medicine initiative in Kumasi, Ghana: application of Lean manufacturing principals to low-resource health systems. Academic Emergency Medicine, Vol. 19 n°.3, pp. 338-347, 2012.

CEVIKCAN, E.; DURMUSOGLU, M. B. **An integrated job release and scheduling approach on parallel machines: An application in electric wire-harness industry.** Computers & Industrial Engineering, Vol. 76, pp. 318-332, 2014.

CHEN, J. C.; LI, Y.; SHADY, B. D. **From value stream mapping toward a lean/sigma continuous improvement process: an industrial case study.** International Journal of Production Research. Vol. 8 n°.4, pp. 1069-1086, 2010.

CHEN, K. M.; CHEN, J. C.; COX, R. A. **Real time facility performance monitoring system using RFID technology.** Assembly Automation, Vol. 32 n°.2, pp. 185-196, 2012.

CHEN, J. C.; CHENG, C. H.; HUANG, P. B. **Supply chain management with lean production and RFID application: A case study.** Expert Systems with Applications, Vol. 40 n°.9, pp. 3389-3397, 2013.

CHEN, J. C.; CHENG, C.; HUANG, P. T. B.; WANG, K. J.; HUANG, C.; TING, T. **Warehouse management with lean and RFID application: a case study.** The International Journal of Advanced Manufacturing Technology, Vol. 69 n°.1⁄4, pp. 531542, 2013.

CHIARINI, A. **Risk management and cost reduction of cancer drugs using Lean Six Sigma tools.** Leadership in Health Services, Vol. 25 n°.4, pp. 318-330, 2012.

CHIARINI, A. **Waste savings in patient transportation inside large hospitals using lean thinking tools and logistic solutions.** Leadership in Health Services, Vol. 26 n°.4, pp. 356-367, 2013.

CHIARINI, A. **Sustainable manufacturing-greening processes using specific Lean Production tools: an empirical observation from European motorcycle component manufacturers.** Journal of Cleaner Production, Vol. 85, pp. 226-233, 2014.

CIMA, R. R.; BROWN, M. J.; HEBL, J. R.; MOORE, R.; ROGERS, J. C.; KOLLENGODE, A.; AMSTUTZ, G. J.; WEISBROD, C. A.; NARR, B. J.; DESCHAMPS, C. **Use of lean and six sigma methodology to improve operating room efficiency in a high-volume tertiary-care academic medical center.** Journal of the American College of Surgeons, Vol. 213, n°.1, pp. 83-92, 2011.

CLASON, D. L.; DORMODY, T. J. **Analyzing data measured by individual likert-type items.** Journal of Agricultural Education, Vol. 35 n°.4, pp. 31-35, 1993.

COOKSON, D.; READ, C.; MUKHERJEE, P.; COOKE, M. **Improving the quality of emergency department care by removing waste using lean value stream mapping.** International Journal of Clinical Leadership, Vol. 17 n°.1, pp. 25-30, 2011.

COOPER, H. C. **Research synthesis and meta-analysis: A step-by-step approach.** Thousand Oaks, 2010.

CORRÊA, H.; GIANESI, I. G. N. **Just in time, MRP II e OPT: um enfoque estratégico.** Sao Paulo: Editora Atlas, 1994.

DURANIK, T.; RUZBARSKY, J.; STOPPER, M. **Using VSM method to increase value creation in manual production system.** DAAAM International Scientific Book, pp. 565-572, 2012.

EBSCO. **About Ebsco.** 2015. Available at: <https://www.ebsco.com/about>. Accessed on: April 11, 2015.

ELSEVIER. **About Elsevier.** 2001. Available at :<

http://www.elsevier.com.br/site/institucional/Default.aspx>. Accessed on: April 11, 2015.

EMERALD GROUP PUBLISHING. **About Emerald**. 2015. Available at: < http://www.emeraldgrouppublishing.com/about/index.htm>. Accessed on: April 11, 2015.

FAULKNER, W.; BADURDEEN, F. **Sustainable value stream mapping (Sus-**

VSM): methodology to visualize and assess manufacturing sustainability performance. Journal of Cleaner Production, Vol. 85, pp. 8-18, 2014.

FERRO, J. R. **The essence of the value stream mapping tool.** 2005. Available at:<http://www.lean.org.br/artigos/61/a-essencia-da-ferramenta-mapping-the-flow-of-value.aspx>. Accessed on: February 10, 2015.

FERRO, J. R.; SHOOK, J.; KOSAKA, G.; COACH, G. **Lean Institute Brasil.** 2010. Available at: <http://www.lean.org.br/leanmail/89/desdobramento-da-estrategia-na-gestao-lean.aspx>. Accessed on: February 10, 2015.

FILIPPINI, R. **Operations management research: some reflections on evolution, models and empirical studies in OM.** International Journal of Operations and Production Management, Vol. 17 n°.7, pp. 655-670, 1997.

FLEISS, J. L. **Measuring nominal scale agreement among many raters.** Psychological Bulletin, Vol. 76 n°.5, pp. 378-382, 1971.

FLEISS, J. L. **Statistical methods for rates and proportions.** New York: Wiley, 1981.

FOLINAS, D.; AIDONIS, D.; TRIANTAFILLOUA, D.; MALINDRETOSB, G. **Exploring the greening of the food supply chain with lean thinking techniques.** Procedia Technology, Vol. 8, pp. 416-424, 2013.

FORZA, C. **Survey research in operations management: a processbased perspective.** International Journal of Operations & Production Management, Vol. 22 n°.2, pp. 152-194, 2002.

GARDNER, J. T.; COOPER, M C. **Strategic supply chain mapping approaches**. Journal of Business Logistics, Ohio, vol.24, n..2, 2003.

GARG, A. K.; NAIDO, M. S. **Lean manufacturing as an alternative operational process in a small printing organization in johannesburg**. Pakistan Journal of Social Sciences, Vol. 32 n°.2, pp. 395-410, 2012.

GARRET, D. F.; LEE, J. **Lean construction submittal process-a case study.**

Quality Engineering, Vol. 23 n°.1, pp. 84-93, 2011.

GIBBONS, P. M.; KENNEDY, C.; BURGESS, S. C.; GODFREY, P. **The development of a lean resource mapping framework: introducing an 8th waste.** International Journal of Lean Six Sigma, Vol. 3 n°.1, pp. 4-27, 2012.

GIL, A. C. **Como elaborar projectos de pesquisa.** Sao Paulo: Atlas, 1996.

GROVE, A. L.; MEREDITH, J. O.; MACINTYRE, M.; ANGELIS, J.; NEAILEY, K.

Lean implementation in primary care health visiting services in National Health Service UK. Quality Safety Health Care, Vol. 19 n°.43, pp. 1-5, 2010.

GURUMURTHY, A.; KODALI, R. **Design of lean manufacturing systems using value stream mapping with simulation: A case study.** Journal of Manufacturing Technology Management, Vol. 22 n°4, pp. 444-473, 2011.

HADID, W.; MANSOURI, S. A. **The lean-performance relationship in services: a theoretical model.** International Journal of Operations & Production Management, Vol. 34 n°.6, pp. 750-785, 2014.

HAEFNER, B.; KRAEMER, A.; STAUSS, T.; LANZA, G. **Quality value stream mapping.** Procedia CIRP, Vol. 17, pp. 254-259, 2014.

HAYES, A. F.; KRIPPENDORF, K. **Answering the call for a standard reliability measure for coding data.** Communication Methods and Measures, Vol. 1, No.1, pp. 77-89, 2007.

HEINZEN, M.; METTLER, S.; CORADI, A.; BOUTELLIER; R. **A new application of value-stream mapping in new drug development: a case study within Novartis.** Drug Discovery Today, pp. 1-5, 2014.

HINES, P.; RICH, N. **The seven value stream mapping tools.** International Journal of Operations & Production Management, Vol. 17 n.1, pp. 46-64, 1997.

HINES, P.; RICH, N.; BICHENO, J.; BRUNT, D.; TAYLOR, D.; BUTTERWORTH, C.; SULLIVAN, J. **Value stream management.** The

International Journal of Logistics Management, Vol. 9 n.1, pp. 25-42, 1998.

HINES, P.; RICH, N. ESAIN, A. **Value stream mapping: a distribution industry application**. Benchmarking: An International Journal, Vol. 6 n°.1, pp. 60-77, 1999.

HOFACKER, A.; SANTOS, A.; SANTOS, A. P. L. **A critical view of the public procurement process in Germany.** Built Environment, Vol. 12 n°.3, pp. 45-56, 2012.

HOLWEG, M. **The three dimensions of responsiveness.** International Journal of Operations & Production Management, Vol. 25 n°7, pp. 603-622, 2005.

HOPAYIAN, K. **The need for caution in interpreting high quality systematic reviews.** Education and Debate, Vol. 323, pp. 681-684, 2001.

HUANG, C. C.; LIU, S. H. **A novel approach to lean control for Taiwan-funded enterprises in mainland china**. International Journal of Production Research, Vol. 43 n°.12, pp. 2553-2575, 2005.

HYDES, T.; HANSI, N.; TREBBLE, T. M. **Lean thinking transformation of the unsedated upper gastrointestinal endoscopy pathway improves efficiency and is associated with high leves of patient satisfaction**. BMJ Quality & Safety, Vol. 21 n°.1, pp 2-14, 2012.

JASTI, N. V. K.; SHARMA, A. **Lean manufacturing implementation using value stream mapping as a tool: A case study from auto components industry.** International Journal of Lean Six Sigma, Vol. 5 n°.1, pp. 89-116, 2014.

JIMÉNEZ, E.; TEJEDA, A.; MARTiNEZ, E.; PÉREZ, M.; BLANCO, J. **Applicability of lean production with VSM to the Rioja wine sector**. International Journal of Production Research, Vol. 50 n°.7, pp. 1890-1904, 2012.

KAALE, R. L.; SEE, D. D.; MESSNER, K.; EITEL, D. R.; JOHNSON, D. E.; MCKNIFF, S.; AMSTERDAM, J. T.; FALVO, T. P.; STIKE, R. L.; GROVE, L.;

SNYDER, K. C. **Time value stream mapping as a tool to measure patient flow through emergency department triage.** Annals of Emergency Medicine, Vol. 46

n°. 3, pp. 108, 2005.

KHURUM, M.; PETERSEN, K.; GORSCHEK, T. **Extending value stream mapping through waste definition beyond customer perspective.** Journal of Software: Evolution and Process, Vol. 26 n°12, pp. 1074-1105, 2014.

KOCAKULAH, M. C.; UPSON, J. **Cost analysis of computerized physician order entry using value stream analysis: a case study.** Research in Healthcare Financial Management, Vol. 10 n°.1, p. 13, 2005.

KOSAKA, G. **Lean Institute Brasil.** 2015. Available at: <http://www.lean.org.br/colunas/13/Gilberto-Kosaka.aspx> Accessed on: February 18, 2015.

KRIPPENDORF, K. **Content analysis: An introduction to its methodology.** Thousand Oaks, California: Sage, 2004a.

KRIPPENDORF, K. **Reliability in content analysis: some common misconceptions and recommendations.** Humans Communication Research, Vol. 30 n°.3, pp. 411-433, 2004b.

KRIPPENDORF, K. **Computing Krippendorff's alpha-reliability.** Philadelphia: Annenberg School for Communication Departmental Papers, 2011.

KUHLANG, P.; EDTMAYR, T.; SIHN, W. **Methodical approach to increase productivity and reduce *lead time* in assembly and production-logistic processes.** CIRP Journal of Manufacturing Science and Technology, Vol. 4 n°.1, pp. 24-32, 2011.

L'HOMMEDIEU, T.; KAPPELER, K. **Lean methodology in i.v. medication processes in a children's hospital.** American Journal of Heath-System Pharmacy, Vol. 67 n°.24, pp. 2115-2118, 2010.

LASA, S. I.; LABURU, C. O.; VILA, R. C. **An evaluation of the value stream mapping tool.** Business Process Management Journal, Vol. 14 n°.1, pp. 39-52, 2008.

LAWRENCE, F. B.; KRISHNADEVARAJAN, P.; CHIDAMBARAM, M.;

VENKATACHALAM, V. V. **Becoming lean - roadmap and implementation.** Electronic and Industrial Distribution Industries, Vol, 1 n°.1, pp. 25-39, 2007.

LIAN, Y. H.; VAN LANDEGHEM, H. **Analyzing the effects of lean manufacturing using a value stream mapping-based simulation generator.** International Journal of Production Research. Vol. 45 n°.13, pp. 3037-3058, 2007.

LIBRELATO, T. P.; LACERDA, D. P.; RODRIGUES, L. H.; VEIT, D. R. **A process improvement approach based on the Value Stream Mapping and the Theory of Constraints Thinking Process.** Business Process Management Journal, Vol. 20 n°.6, pp. 922-949, 2014.

LIKER, J. K.; CONVIS, G. L. **The Toyota lean leadership model - how to achieve and sustain excellence through leadership development**. 1ed. s.l.:Bookman, 2013.

LIMA, M. L. S. C.; ZAWSLAK, P. A. **Lean production as a differentiating factor in the supply capacity of SMEs.** Gestao da Produçâo, Vol. 13 n°. 2, pp. 5769, 2003.

LU, J. C.; WANG, C. Y.; YANG, T. **A lean pull system design analyzed by value stream mapping and multiple criteria decision-making method under demand uncertainty**. International Journal of Computer Integrated Manufacturing, Vol. 24 n°.3, pp. 211-228, 2011.

LUMMUS, R. R.; VOKURKA, R. J.; RODEGHIERO, B. **Improving quality through value stream mapping: A case study of a physician's clinic.** Total Quality Management & Business Excellence, Vol. 17 n°.8, pp. 1063-1075, 2006.

MARCHWINSKI, C. **State of lean report**. Available at: <http://www.lean.org>, 2004.

MARQUES, A. F.; ALVES, A. C.; SOUSA, J. P. **An Approach for integrated design of flexible production systems.** Procedia CIRP, Vol. 7, pp. 586-591, 2013.

MATT, D. T. **Template based production system design.** Journal of Manufacturing Technology Management, Vol. 19 n°7, pp. 783-797, 2008.

MATT, D.; KRAUSE, D.; RAUCH, R. **Adaptation of the value stream**

optimization approach to collaborative company networks in the construction industry. Procedia CIRP, Vol. 12, pp. 402-407, 2013.

MATT, D. T. **Adaptation of the value stream mapping approach to the design of lean engineer-to-order production systems: A case study.** Journal of Manufacturing Technology Management, Vol. 25 n°.3, pp. 334-350, 2014.

MATTAR, F. N. **Pesquisa de marketing: metodologia e planejamento.** Sao Paulo: Atlas, 1996.

MC DONALD, T.; VAN AKEN, E. M.; RENTES, A. F.X. **Utilizing simulation to enhance value stream mapping: a manufacturing case application.** Institute Journal Logistic Research Apply, Vol. 5 n°.2, pp. 213-232, 2002.

MIGUEL, P. A. C. **Case study in production engineering: structuring and recommendations for its conduct.** Produçâo, Vol. 17 n°.1, pp. 216-229, 2007.

MOHANTY, R. P.; YADAY, O. P.; JAIN, R. **Implementation of lean manufacturing principles in auto industry.** Vilakshan, XIMB Journal of Management, pp. 1-32, 2007.

MÜLLER, E.; SCHILLIG, R.; STOCK, T.; SCHMEILER, M. **Improvement of injection molding processes by using dual energy signatures.** Procedia CIRP, Vol. 17, pp. 704-709, 2014.

NEPAL, B.; NATARAJARATHINAM, M.; BALLA, K. **Improving manufacturing process for biomedical products: a case study.** Journal of Manufacturing Technology Management, Vol. 22 n°4, pp. 527-540, 2011.

NEUENDORF, K. A. **The content analysis guidebook.** Thousand Oaks, California: Sage Publications, 2002.

NG, D.; VAIL, G.; THOMAS, S.; SCHMIDT, N. **Applying the lean principles of the Toyota Production System to reduce wait times in the emergency department.** Canadian journal of emergency medicine, Vol. 12 n°.1, pp. 50-57, 2010.

NORONHA, D. P.; FERREIRA, S. M. S. P. **Literature Reviews.** 2000.

OLIVEIRA, A. O.; PHILIPPI, D. A. ***Lead time* reduction strategies: a case study at the porto dos sonhos factory**. SIMPOI, pp. 1-16, 2013.

PAVNASKAR, S. J.; GERSHENSON, J. K.; JAMBEKAR, A. B. **Classification scheme for lean manufacturing tools.** International Journal of Production Research, Vol. 41 n.13, pp. 3075-3090, 2003.

POJASEK, R. B. **Mapping information flow the production process.** Environmental Quality Manager. South Carolina, vol.13, n.3; p.89, mar.-mai, 2004.

PRASHAR, A. **Redesigning an assembly line through Lean-Kaizen: an Indian case.** The TQM Journal, Vol. 26 n°.5, pp. 475-498, 2014.

RAHANI, A. R.; AL-ASHRAF, M. **Production flow analysis through value stream mapping: A lean manufacturing process case study**. Procedia Engineering, Vol. 41, pp. 1727-1734, 2012.

ROLDAN, F.; MIYAKE, D. I. **Forecast changes in the automotive industry: initiatives for structuring decision-making processes and information processing.** Gestao e Produçâo, Vol. 11 n°.3, pp. 413-427, 2004.

ROTHER, M.; SHOOK, J. **Learning to see: value stream mapping to ass value and eliminate.** Cambridge, MA: Lean Enterprise Institute, 1998.

SALGADO, E. G.; MELLO, C. H. P.; SILVA, C. E. S.; OLIVEIRA, E. S.; ALMEIDA, D. A. **Analysis of the application of value stream mapping in identifying waste in the product development process.** Gestao e Produçao, Vol. 16 n.3, 2009.

SCHWARZ, P.; PANNES, K. D.; NATHAN, M.; REIMER, H. J.; KLEESPIES, A.; KUHN, N.; RUPP, A.; ZÜGEL, N. P. **Lean processes for optimizing OR capacity utilization: prospective analysis before and after implementation of value stream mapping (VSM).** Langenbeck's Archives of Surgery, Vol. 396 n°.7, pp. 1047-1053, 2011.

SCIELO. Scielo Model - **Electronic publishing model for developing countries.** 2000. Available at <http://www.scielo.org/php/level.php>. Accessed on: April 11, 2015.

SCIELO. **Scielo Model - Electronic publishing model for developing countries.** 2000. Available at:

< http://www.scielo.org/php/level.php?component=56&item=1&lang=pt>. Accessed on: April 11, 2015.

SERRANO, L.; OCHOA, C.; CASTRO, R. **Evaluation of value stream mapping in manufacturing system redesign.** International Journal of Production Research, Vol.46 n°.16, pp. 4409-4430, 2008.

SETH, D.; SETH, N.; GOEL, D. **Application of value stream mapping (VSM) for minimization of wastes in the processing side of supply chain of cottonseed oil industry in Indian context.** Journal of Manufacturing Technology Management, Vol. 19 n°.4, pp. 529-550, 2008.

SHINGO, S. **The Toyota Production System: from a production engineering point of view**. Porto Alegre: Bookman, 1996a.

SHINGO, S. **Zero-stock production systems: the Shingo System for continuous improvement.** Porto Alegre: Bookman, 1996b.

SINGH, R. K.; KUMAR, S.; CHOUDHURY, K.; TIWARIS, M. K. **Lean tool selection in a die casting unit: a fuzzy-based decision support heuristic.** International journal of production research, Vol. 44 n°.7, pp. 1399-1429, 2006.

SINGH, B.; SHARMA, S. K. **Value stream mapping as a versatile tool for lean implementation: an Indian case study of a manufacturing firm**. Measuring Business Excellence, Vol. 13, n°.3, pp. 58-68, 2009.

SINGH, B. S. K. G.; SHARMA, S; GREWAL, C. **Lean implementation and its benefits to production industry.** International Journal of Lean Six Sigma, Vol. 1 n°.2, pp. 157-168, 2010.

SINGH, B., GARG, S. K.; SHARMA, S. K. **Value stream mapping: literature review and implications for Indian industry.** The International Journal of Advanced Manufacturing Technology, Vol. 53 n°. 5-8, pp. 799-809, 2011.

SINGH, H.; SINGH, A. **Application of lean manufacturing using value stream mapping in an auto-parts manufacturing unit.** Journal of Advances in Management Research, Vol.10 n°.1, pp. 72-84, 2013.

SLACK, N. **Production Management**. Sao Paulo: Atlas, 1999.

SOUZA, R. P.; HÉKIS, H. R.; OLIVEIRA, L. A. B.; QUEIROZ, F. C. B. P.; VALENTIM, R. A. M. **Implementation of a six sigma project in a 3M division of Brazil.** International Journal of Quality & Reliability Management, Vol. 30 n°.2, pp. 129-141, 2013.

STORCH, R. L.; LIM, S. **Improving flow to achieve lean manufacturing in shipbuilding.** Production Planning & Control, Vol.10 n°.2, pp. 127-137, 1999.

SULLiVAN, W. G.; MC DONALD, T. N.; VAN AKEN, E. M. **Equipment replacement decisions and lean manufacturing.** Robotics and Computer Integrated Manufacturing, Vol. 18, pp. 255-265, 2002.

SUSILAWATI, A.; TAN, J. BELL, D.; SARWAR, M. **Fuzzy logic based method to measure degree of lean activity in manufacturing industry.** Journal of Manufacturing Systems, Vol. 34, pp. 1-11, 2015.

TABANLI, R. M.; ERTAY, T. **Value stream mapping and benefit-cost analysis application for value visibility of a pilot project on RFID investment integrated to a manual production control system - a case study.** International Journal Advanced Manufacturing Technology, Vol. 66 n°.5/8, pp. 987-1002, 2013.

TANCO, M.; SANTOS, J.; RODRIGUEZ, J. L.; REICH, J. **Applying lean techniques to nougat fabrication: a seasonal case study.** The International Journal of Advanced Manufacturing Technology, Vol. 68 n°5/8, pp. 1639-1654, 2013.

TEICHGRABER, U. K.; DE BUCOURT, M. **Applying value stream mapping techniques to eliminate non-value-added waste for the procurement of**

endovascular stents. European Journal of Radiology, Vol. 81 n°.1, pp. 47-52, 2012.

THIOLLENT, M. **Action Research Methodology**. Sao Paulo: Atlas, 1997.

THOMÉ, A. M. T.; HOLLMANN, R. L.; SCAVARDA, L. F. **Research synthesis in collaborative planning forecast and replenishment.** Industrial Management & Data Systems, Vol. 114 n°.6, pp. 949-965, 2014.

THOMÉ, A.; SCAVARDA, L. F.; FERNANDEZ, N.; SCAVARDA, A. J. **Sales and operations planning: A research synthesis.** International Journal of Production, Vol. 4 n°.1, pp. 1-13, 2012a.

THOMÉ, A.; SCAVARDA, L. F.; FERNANDEZ, N.; SCAVARDA, A. J. **Sales and operations planning and the firm performance.** International Journal of Productivity and Performance Management, Vol. 61 n°.4, pp. 359-381, 2012b.

TYAGI, S.; CHOUDHARY, A.; CAI, X.; YANG, K. **Value stream mapping to reduce the lead-time of product development process.** International Journal of Production Economics, Vol. 160, pp. 202-212, 2014.

VIEIRA, M. G. **Application of value stream mapping to evaluate a production system.** Dissertation submitted to the Federal University of Santa Catarina for a Master's Degree in Mechanical Engineering. UFSA. Postgraduate Program in Mechanical Engineering. 2006.

VINODH, S.; ARVIND, K.; SOMANAATHAN, M. **Application of value stream mapping in an Indian camshaft manufacturing organization.** Journal of Manufacturing Technology Management, Vol. 21 n°.7, pp. 888-900, 2010.

VINODH, S.; SOMANAATHAN, M. R.; ARVIND, K. **Development of value stream map for achieving leanness in a manufacturing organization.** Journal of Engineering, Design and Technology, Vol. 11 n°2, pp. 129-141, 2013.

VLACHOS, L.; BOGDANOVIC, **A Lean thinking in the european hotel industry.** Tourism Management, Vol. 36, pp. 354-363, 2013.

WALTER, O. M. F. C.; TUBINO, D. F. **Methods for evaluating the**

implementation of lean manufacturing: a literature review and classification. Gestao Produçâo, Vol. 20 n°.1, pp. 23-45, 2013.

WANG, C.; QUESADA-PINEDA, H.; KLINE, D. E.; BUEHLMANN, U. **Using value stream mapping to analyze an upholstery furniture engineering process.** Forest Products Journal, Vol. 61 n°.5, p. 411, 2011.

WANG, P.; MOHAMED, Y.; ABOURIZK, S.; RAWA, A. **Flow production of pipe spool fabrication: simulation to support implementation of lean technique.** Journal of Construction Engineering and Management, Vol. 135 n°.10, pp. 1027-1038, 2009.

WEE, H. M.; WU, S. **Lean supply chain and its effect on product cost and quality: a case study on Ford Motor Company.** Supply Chain Management: An International Journal, Vol. 14 n°.5, pp. 335-341, 2009.

WOMACK, J. P.; JONES, D. T. **Lean thinking banish waste and create wealth in your corporation.** London, Touchstone Books, 1996.

WONG, R.; LEVI, A. W.; HARIGOPAL, M.; SCHOFIELD, K.; CHHIENG, D. C. **The Positive impact of simultaneous implementation of the BD focalpoint GS imaging system and lean principles on the operation of gynecologic cytology**. Arch Pathol Lab Med, Vol. 136, 2012.

XIE, Y.; PENG, Q. **Integration of value stream mapping and agent-based modeling for OR improvement.** Business Process Management Journal, Vol. 18 n°.4, pp. 585599, 2012.

YANG, T.; LU, J. C. **The use of a multiple attribute decision-making method and value stream mapping in solving the pacemaker location problem**. International Journal of Production Research, Vol. 49 n°.10, pp. 2793-2817, 2011.

YIN, R. K. **Case study - planning and method.** 2 ed. Sao Paulo: Bookman, 2010.

YU, H.; TWEED, T.; AL-HUSSEIN, M.; NASSERI, R. **Development of lean model for house construction using value stream mapping.** Journal of Construction Engineering and Management, Vol. 135 n°.8, pp. 782-790, 2009.

YU, H.; AL-HUSSEIN, M.; ASCE, M.; AL-JIBOURI, S.; TELYAS, A. **Lean transformation in a modular building company: a case for implementation.** Journal of Management in Engineering, Vol. 29 n°.1, pp. 103-111, 2013.

7. Appendices

7.1. Appendix A - Description of the type of study

7.1.1. Case studies

The case study is an empirical investigation of a contemporary phenomenon within a well-defined real-life context (a program, a company, a business process or a production or logistics process) (Yin, 2010). It involves an in-depth analysis of one or more objects (cases), in order to provide a broad and detailed understanding (Gil, 1996; Berto & Nakano, 2000).

Its aim is to deepen knowledge about a problem that is not sufficiently defined (Mattar, 1996), in order to stimulate understanding, suggest hypotheses and questions or develop theory (Miguel, 2007). The main trend in all types of case study is that they try to clarify why a decision or set of decisions were made, how they were implemented and with what results they achieved (Yin, 2010).

7.1.2. Research study - *survey*

The *survey involves collecting* data from a significant sample about a problem to be studied and then, by means of quantitative analysis, obtaining the conclusions corresponding to the data collected (Gil, 1996).

Surveys aim to contribute to knowledge in a particular area of interest by collecting information about individuals or their environments (Forza, 2002).

According to Forza (2002) a *survey* can be classified as: (i) exploratory, where it takes place in the early stages of research into a given phenomenon, when the aim is to acquire an initial view of a given topic and provide a basis for a more detailed survey; (ii) descriptive, where it is aimed at understanding the relevance of a certain phenomenon, describing its distribution in the population. Its aim is not to develop a theory, but it can provide input for building theories or refining them, and; (iii) confirmatory, which occurs when knowledge about a phenomenon has already been developed theoretically using well-defined concepts (constructs), models and propositions. Thus, they are characterized as testing theories or as explanatory.

Generally speaking, the structure of a *survey* is basically subdivided into the following stages: *(i)* development of a conceptual theoretical model and constructs; (*ii)* characterization of the population and sample; (*iii)* preparation of the data collection instrument; (*iv)* data collection and evaluation of the rate of return and; *(v)* data analysis and interpretation of the results (Gil, 1996*)*.

7.1.3. Mathematical model

Modeling is the use of mathematical techniques to describe the functioning of a system or part of a production system (Berto & Nakano, 2000).

7.1.4. Action research

Action research is a type of empirically-based research that is designed and carried out in close association with an action or the resolution of a collective problem and in which researchers and participants representing the situation or problem are involved in a cooperative or participatory way (Thiollent, 1997).

7.1.5. Literature review

Literature reviews are an important activity for identifying, getting to know and monitoring the development of research in a particular area of knowledge (Noronha & Ferreira, 2000), as well as enabling coverage of a range of phenomena that is generally broader than that which could be researched directly (Gil, 1996). In addition, reviews allow the identification of perspectives for future research, contributing with suggestions of ideas for the development of new research projects (Noronha & Ferreira, 2000).

7.1.6. Simulation

Simulation consists of using techniques to simulate the operation of production systems, based on a set of variables in a given domain, in order to investigate the causal and quantitative relationship between these variables (Bertrand & Fransoo, 2002).

7.1.7. Multi-method

When the study is based on two types of study, the approach is defined as multi-method (Walter & Tubino, 2013).

7.2. Appendix B - Type of information collected in the articles selected for the VSM study

Description of the information collected in the articles selected for the VSM study

N°	Database	Author	Year of publication	Title
Magazine	Magazine acronym	Parents	Type of study	Type of industry
Type of sector	No. of units observed	Type of interviewed	Type of VSM	Tools used
Motivation research	Application area VSM	Type of production	Tools used	Data collection
Objectives established	Product family	Losses identified	Team selected	Planning of *kaizens*
Execution of *kaizens*	Current status map	State map future	Type of result	Description result
Research limitations				

Printed by Books on Demand GmbH, Norderstedt / Germany